9780706351224

D1785121

RED GUIDE

The Peak District

Buxton, Bakewell
Matlock, Chatsworth
Ashborne, Dovedale

Edited by Reginald J. W. Hammond

Fifth edition

WARD, LOCK & CO., LIMITED
LONDON AND MELBOURNE

This Guide covers the Derbyshire Peak District and includes the principal touring centres of Buxton and Matlock.

For convenience of local sale it is available bound up under each of the following titles:

The Peak District
Matlock and the Peak District
Buxton and the Peak District

Printed in Great Britain by Northumberland Press Ltd., Gateshead on Tyne

CONTENTS

CONTENTS

ILLUSTRATIONS

INTRODUCTION

The Peak and the Lows—The National Park—Rail and Road Routes—Motoring and Cycling—Youth Hostels—Hotels and Accommodation

The region described in this guide is one of the most picturesque and interesting in Great Britain. Measuring 80 miles from north to south, and 60 miles across at its widest part, it extends from the southern extremity of the Pennine range to Ashbourne. From Buxton, excellent roads, with bus services, radiate throughout the area, and this is a good centre from which to explore the northern uplands. Ashbourne is a favourite starting point for Dovedale and the Manifold valley. To the south-east, Matlock is convenient for visiting the lower reaches of the Derwent valley, Darley dale, and the rock-climbing districts. Bakewell is well situated for the central dales, and for visiting Haddon Hall and Chatsworth. The villages of Edale and Hayfield are gateways to Kinder Scout, and Hope and Castleton are convenient for the upper Derwent valley and for the great caverns of Peakland.

Origin of the name

The word " Peak " is misleading, since there is no sharply pointed hill. The name is applied to the whole area, and may be a derivation from the name of some early colonists— the *Pecsaete* or *Peacs*. The few peaks in the area are usually termed *tors* or *pikes*, and the uplands are plateaux or hills with gently rounded summits. Similarly the word " low " as part of a place name, e.g. Bleaklow Head, Grin Low, does not refer to the height, but is derived from the Saxon word *hlow* meaning a covering, and probably indicates an ancient burial place. Many of the Derbyshire hills with names ending in *low* have been examined, and skeletons, arrow heads and other relics have been found in nearly all of them.

INTRODUCTION

The grandeur and beauty of these highland regions, giving spacious views of plateaux and moorland, are matched by the charm and loveliness of the dales. Some of these are narrow and precipitous, but clad with foliage and so winding and land-locked that they seem to possess their own sky; others are broad, flat and verdant. Although much of the district is accessible by car, it is only by walking that the most enchanting spots can be discovered. Numerous footpaths, by-lanes, field walks and moorland ways offer delightful routes, varying from the strenuous going over moors and hills to the gentle meandering through the soft dales.

The unspoiled beauty of the Peak District owes much of its preservation to the safeguarding efforts of voluntary workers and unofficial bodies. In 1951 much of this region was recognized to be one of Britain's premier landscape areas when it was chosen as the first—

National Park

The Peak District National Park comprises an area of some 542 square miles. It extends northward to Kinder, Bleaklow and Holme Moss, and southward to Tissington, the enchanting Dovedale, and the Manifold valley. Eastward it encloses the architectural gems of Haddon Hall and Chatsworth, with the ancient town of Bakewell as the principal town in the National Park. Westward is the wooded valley of the Dane and the River Goyt, and the high view-points of Shuttlingsloe and Shining Tor.

A very active Peak Park Planning Board has its offices at Aldern House, Bakewell, and maintains Information Centres at Fieldhead in the village of Edale and at St. Ann's Well in the Crescent at Buxton. The Edale centre specializes in serving the needs of walkers on the nearby moorlands, but both information centres are equipped with maps, photo-graphs and other displays of interest to visitors, and publica-tions about the National Park are available. A caravan has been equipped as a mobile information centre and is stationed at places where visitors congregate in large numbers during the summer months.

The Board have completed many schemes for the preservation and enhancement of the beauty of the Peak District and have others under consideration—tree planting, construction of inconspicuous car parks, lay-bys and caravan sites and removal of unsightly buildings. They control advertisements and building development and have fostered the use of stone in local buildings which is so distinctive a feature of the Peak District. The Board have devoted special care to the provision of access to the high moorlands of the Kinder Scout and Bleaklow area where previously walkers had no right of access. Access agreements have now been made in respect of some 43 square miles of open country and further areas are under negotiation.

A service of voluntary wardens, under the direction of the Board's Head Warden, patrols the Kinder plateau and other areas, to assist visitors and to prevent damage. Not only are walkers helped, but during severe weather sheep are rescued and practical assistance given to farmers. These services have helped to foster good relationships between residents and visitors. And visitors themselves can help by bearing in mind that although this area is now a National Park the land has not been "nationalized," and that they have no right to roam at will over farmland or other property which is private. They should be mindful of their responsibilities and avoid doing any damage. All are asked to guard against causing fires; to avoid damaging walls or fences; to remember to fasten gates; to leave no litter; to keep to the paths, and to protect the life of the countryside so that its beauties are preserved for future generations.

ROUTES TO THE DISTRICT

By Rail

The Peak District is well served by rail from all parts of Britain. It is connected with London and the South by the London Midland Region line, the journey taking 3–3½ hours. From St. Pancras the route is *viâ* Derby, Matlock, Bakewell and Miller's Dale; from here a branch line goes to Buxton.

The Matlocks have two stations. *Matlock* is the principal station, nearly all express trains stopping here. *Matlock Bath*, a mile farther south, is served by local trains. Passengers for Bakewell, conveniently situated for visits to Chatsworth House and Haddon Hall, travel by local trains.

The Eastern Region line from Chesterfield runs southward to join the Derby–Matlock route at Ambergate. From Sheffield, a branch line from *Dore* runs through the Derwent valley to Hope, Edale and Chinley.

From the west, the line from Manchester to Sheffield serves the north side of the Peak *viâ* Penistone and Glossop, and another line terminates at Hayfield. Diesel-engined trains link Manchester with Buxton.

By Road

There are express **coach services** from many of the larger towns.

For **motorists** the most direct routes from London are the M1 to Northampton, then A508 to join the A6 at Market Harborough, or the A6 throughout to the latter place. Thence A6 to Leicester, Derby, Matlock, Bakewell and Buxton.

For those who prefer a more leisurely and attractive route, avoiding congested areas, the following is recommended:—

Leave London by the A40 to Hanger Lane station. Cross Western Avenue then branch left (A4005) towards Sudbury. Follow the Watford Road A409 to Harrow and Wealdstone, and at Hemel

Hempstead follow the B486 to Leighton Buzzard. Leave here by the A418 to Woburn, thence by the A50 and A509 to Wellingborough and Kettering. From Kettering follow the A6003 to Uppingham, the A606 to Melton Mowbray, and join the A60 then A52 into Nottingham. Continue by the A52 to Derby, and leave Derby by the A6 for Matlock, Bakewell and Buxton.

The following is a delightful return route. Leave Buxton by the A515 to Ashbourne and Sudbury, and at Lichfield fork keep left. Enter and leave Lichfield by the A51, then bear right to A446, which joins the A452 to enter Kenilworth, and from here take the A46 to Warwick. Leave by the A41, which runs through Banbury, Bicester and Aylesbury. From here, cross the Chilterns by the A413 to Amersham and Chalfont St. Peter. About two miles beyond Chalfont turn left along A40 for London.

Motoring in the District

Within the Peak District the charm of motoring is its variety; the scenery completely changes within the range of very short car runs. The roads, though hilly, and twisting, have good surfaces, are well sign-posted, and there are few really steep gradients.

Suggested Car Drives of about 50-60 miles

1. Matlock to Chatsworth, Eyam, Hope, Castleton, Edale and the Peak National Park.
2. Matlock to Buxton *viâ* Bakewell, Haddon Hall, return *viâ* Monyash, Arbor Low, Youlgreave, Winster, Cromford.
3. Buxton to Earl Sterndale, Alstonfield, Ashbourne, return *viâ* Tissington and Hartington.
4. Over Cat and Fiddle to Macclesfield, Congleton, Moreton Hall, return *viâ* Rudyard Lake, Wincle and Allgreave.
5. Buxton to Leek, thence to Alton Towers (*see* p. 132). Return *viâ* Wootton and Axe Edge.

Cycling

Although many of the roads are hilly, with sharp corners necessitating good brakes, the hardy cyclist is well rewarded by the magnificent views and the attractive villages. For cyclists, the Youth Hostels are a great boon, and there are several delightful routes leading from one hostel to the next.

YOUTH HOSTELS

The Peak District is well provided with Youth Hostels, all in delightful settings. A list is given below. Many of the buildings are modern; others are adapted from manor houses, Tudor halls and country mansions. (For particulars of membership and full information apply *Youth Hostel Association*, Trevelyan House, 8, St. Stephen's Hill, St. Albans, Herts.)

Bretton Hostel, Eyam
Castleton Hall, Castleton (Tel. Hope 235)
Elton Hostel, Main Street, Elton, Matlock
Hartington Hall, Hartington (Tel. Hartington 223)
Ilam Hall, Ilam (Tel. Thorpe Cloud 212)
Leam Hall, Grindleford (Tel. Grindleford 306)
Brunswood Road, Matlock Bath (Tel. Matlock 2983)
Ravenstor, Miller's Dale (Tel. Tideswell 204)
Rowland Cote, Nether Booth, Edale (Tel. Edale 225)
Rudyard Lake, Cliffe Park Hall, Rushton Spencer, Macclesfield (Tel. Rushton Spencer 321)
Sherbrook Lodge, Buxton (Tel. Buxton 1287)
Shining Cliff Hostel, Alderwasley, near Wirksworth

Y.H.A. Regional Office and Shop : 3 Leopold Street, Derby (Tel. 43506).
Y.H.A. Shop : 203 Gibraltar Street, Sheffield 3

HOTELS AND ACCOMMODATION

Alsop-en-le-Dale
New Inns

Ashbourne
Green Man and Black's Head
Station
Royal Oak
Carrington (*Guest House*), Buxton Road

Ashover
Ambervale (*private*)
Country Hotel

Bakewell
Red Lion, The Square
Wheatsheaf
Queen's Arms, Bridge Street
Rutland Arms, The Square
Castle, Bridge Street
Royal Oak, Matlock Street
King's Arms

Manners
Milford House, Mill Street
Peacock

Bamford
Marquis of Granby
Anglers' Rest
Rising Sun

Baslow
Peacock
Devonshire Arms
Rutland Arms

Belper
Lion
George
Midland

Bonsall
Townhead Farm (*Guest House*)

Buxton

Eagle, Market Square
Grove, Grove Parade
Leewood
Old Hall, The Square
Palace
Pendennis, Devonshire Road
Spa
Savoy, Hall Bank
St. Ann's, The Crescent
Argyle, Broad Walk
Buckingham, St. John's Road
Egerton
Griff, Compton Road
Malvern House, Hartington Road
Roseleigh, Broad Walk
Sandringham, Broad Walk
Westminster, Broad Walk
Hawthorn Farm, Fairfield Road

Castleton

Castle
Old Nag's Head
George
Peak
Cheshire Cheese
Bull's Head

Chapel-en-le-Frith

King's Arms
Royal Oak
King's Arms
Roebuck Inn
Beehive Inn, Combs
Oddfellows Inn, Whitehough

Cromford

Greyhound, Market Place

Darley Dale

Whitworth, Dale Road, North
Station, Rowsley

Derby

Clarendon
Midland
Carlton
Friary
Howard
Markeaton
New Inn
Waverley

Gables
York

Edale

Church
Nag's Head

Eyam

Bull's Head
Royal Oak
Miners' Arms

Great Longstone

Crispin
White Lion

Grindleford Bridge

Maynard Arms

Hartington

Charles Cotton
Devonshire Arms

Hathersage

George
Station
Little John

Hayfield

George
Royal
Packhorse
Tunstead (*Guest House*): Kinder

Hope

Old Hall
Idle Hour (*Guest House*)

Ilam (Ashbourne)

Izaak Walton

Leek

Southbank, Southbank Street
Swan
George
Red Lion, Market Place
Rudyard, Rudyard Lake
Three Horse Shoes,
                    Blackshaw Moor

Longnor

Crewe and Harpur Arms

Macclesfield

Angel, Market Place
Bate Hall, Chestergate
Bull's Head, Market Place
George, Jordangate
Macclesfield Arms, Jordangate
Queen's, Albert Place, Waters
 Green
Pack Horse, Jordansgate
Flower Pot, Congleton Road

Mapleton

Temperance

Matlock

High Tor, Dale Road
Crown, Crown Square
Ye Olde English, Dale Road
Queen's, The Bridge
Gate, Smedley Street
Horse Shoe Inn, Matlock Green
King's Head, Church Street
Cavendish (*Guest House*),
 Bank Road
Derwent House (*Boarding*),
 Knowleston Place

Matlock Bath

New Bath, Derby Road
Temple, Temple Walk
Midland, Promenade
George, North Parade
Rutland Arms
Parade View Café, North Parade
Devonshire Café, South Parade
Beehive Café, South Parade
Laurels (*Boarding House*),
 Holme Road

Miller's Dale

Anglers' Rest

Over Haddon

Ivy Dene

Rowsley

Peacock
Station

Taddington

Queen's Arms
Waterloo

Tansley

George and Dragon Inn,
 Nottingham Road

Thorpe

Dog and Partridge
Peveril of the Peak
Hill Crest
Green Farm (Board Residence)

Tideswell

George
Bull's Head

Tissington

Blue Bell
New Inns

Wildboarclough

Crag Inn

Winster

Crown Inn

Wirksworth

George
Red Lion
Hope and Anchor

Youlgreave

Bull's Head
George

THE PEAK DISTRICT

General Description—Geology—History—Natural History—Angling—Rock Climbing—Old Customs

The Peak District is a compact and richly rewarding area not only for the scenic beauty it offers walkers, cyclists and motorists, but also for its importance to those interested in geology, archaeology, natural history, rock climbing, speleology and angling, etc.

Geology

For geologists this is an excellent area to study. The structure, though simple, displays so well the three main factors and processes in the evolution of scenery—elevation, erosion, and different rock formations.

The main mountainous structure, extending from Castleton through Buxton and southwards by the Dove, and along the Derwent valley, consists of **Carboniferous Limestone,** or nearly pure carbonate of lime. This rocky stretch, together with the whole of the Pennine Chain, of which it is the southern end, was formed in ages unknown by a tremendous upheaval from below the sea-level, as is proved by the fact that it is largely composed of the remains of amphibious animals, most of them extinct, of fish, and of shells. It is to this limestone rock, so easily soluble in water, that the varied and romantic beauty of the district is due.

The material is mostly grey in colour, but at Ashford it is dark and is quarried as black marble. A red variety is encountered in a mine at Hartington, and some lighter coloured and brightly ornamented stone is obtained from mines at Ashford and Bakewell. Lead is plentiful throughout the whole formation, the mines having been famous from the time of the Roman occupation; and zinc is met with, although less plentifully. Fluor-spar, a crystal mineral, a combination of lime and fluoric acid, is common in Derbyshire, and forms an important industry through the ornamental articles that are made from it. The most beautiful kind, known as **Blue John**, is more fully referred to on p. 73.

Water charged with carbonic acid has the property of dissolving limestone, and by this action the caverns for which Derbyshire is famous have been formed. (Those around Castleton are unrivalled in Britain.) Indeed, it is not too much to say that, in the ages before historical record, the present lovely vales of the Derwent and the Dove were immense and lengthy caverns, through which the streams flowed, dissolving the rocks around them, until at length the upper crust gave way, and a romantic dale was exposed, growing deeper and wider as the centuries crept on.

In many parts the carboniferous limestone abounds in fossils. Encrinites are found on Grin Low, south of Buxton, and corals at the Miller's Dale end of the road thence to Tideswell. Near Fairfield (Buxton) and in many other places are large deposits of Toadstone (locally Dunstone), the lava of extinct volcanoes. Also claiming a visit for their special features are Chrome Hill, Parkhouse Hill and High Wheeldon, overlooking the upper portion of the Dove valley.

A remarkable phenomenon which can be observed in several places in the more southerly part of the Peak District (notably in the Manifold valley—*see* pp. 147–9) is that of the water swallow—underground channels into which a stream suddenly dives and through which it flows before returning to the surface.

Millstone Grit, formed of beds of sandstone and shale, is the other important feature in the geology of the Peak District. It is impervious to water, and very hard, forming excellent material for building purposes and for mill stones. The Black Rocks, near Matlock, are an example of gritstone. Along the courses of the River Wye and its tributaries are the Yoredale shales.

History and Archaeology

Derbyshire has rich mineral deposits, and it was probably the lead which attracted the first settlers to the area. Archaeologists have found records of Neolithic and Bronze ages. There are long barrows and circles and tumuli, as at Arbor Low.

The Romans have left traces of their roads, many of which converged at Buxton, where the invaders built baths in which to enjoy and utilize the warm, healing waters that still benefit multitudes. The Batham Gate, passing through Peak Forest, and The Street, near Goyt's Bridge, are of Roman origin. Of the period that followed the withdrawal of the Romans there are numerous relics, taken from the caves into which the Britons fled to escape the Picts.

The evidence of Saxon residence is found mainly in the church architecture and in the crosses at Bakewell and Ashbourne. The Norman invaders developed the lead mining, and enclosed almost the whole of Kinder Scout and Bleaklow as a royal hunting forest. William the Conqueror granted lands to William Peveril, who erected the castle on the cliff overlooking what is now the village of Castleton. After Norman times the inhabitants of the Peak District appear to have led a fairly peaceful existence, devoting their days mainly to lead-mining, sheep-farming and drystone-walling.

Natural History

The Peak District has a special interest for botanists. On one side is the flora peculiar to a limestone tract; on the other is the widely different vegetation that flourishes on the gritstone hills and peaty moorlands, and in each division rare flowers are found. Ferns and mosses are present in rich variety, and although fungi are less fully represented than in more wooded parts, a fair number of species may be found, the best hunting-grounds being Dovedale and the Dane Valley.

Over 1,000 species of flowering plants have been recorded for Derbyshire; the Cave Dale at Castleton has a particularly varied flora.

Among the birds of the moors, the red grouse reigns supreme; but there are also snipe, curlew and blackcock, merlin, magpie, jay, pipits, sparrow-hawk, kestrel, while more small birds than can here be named make the moorlands their home. The dipper haunts the mountain streams, and occasionally a heron or kingfisher may be seen. Wagtails, willow-warblers, jackdaws, missel-thrushes and all the swallow tribe favour the limestone dales. Otters prey on the fish in the Dove, and even the badger is not yet extinct. W. H. Hudson devoted three chapters of his *Adventures among Birds* to observations made about Axe Edge.

Monsal Dale, Deep Dale and Combs Lake are most attractive spots for the entomologist, and in the limestone district those interested in shells find many a treasure.

Undoubtedly the best record of Derbyshire birds is the nine-section contribution of the Rev. F. C. R. Jourdain and others to the Journal of the Derbyshire Natural History Society (1908-1917).

The best book authority is F. B. Whitlock's *Birds of Derbyshire*, published in 1893. The earliest is, we believe, Dr. C. Leigh's *Natural History of Lancashire, Cheshire and the Peak of Derbyshire*, published in 1700.

Angling

All the rivers in the area are fishable, but the *Dove*, the *Derwent* and the *Wye* are the principal angling streams. The *Manifold* is also popular. All four are stocked with trout and grayling. Salmon are scarce. Rainbow trout abound in the Wye and the Derwent. Fishing is also available in the Buxton reservoirs—apply Buxton Fly Fishers' Club for tickets. The *Izaak Walton Hotel* at Dovedale controls four miles of both banks of the Dove, and a mile of both banks of the Manifold. Fishing is strictly reserved for hotel residents and is wet and dry fly only. The trout season is March 18th to October 15th; grayling, June 16th to March 18th. There is no charge for grayling fishing after October 15th.

At Alsop-en-le-Dale, the *New Inns Hotel* maintains a long stretch of the Dove, abounding in trout and grayling. Charge is 7s. 6d. per day (to hotel guests) and artificial fly only may be used. Season for trout is March 16th to September 30th. At Hartington, the *Charles Cotton Hotel* controls a stretch of The Dove, and issues tickets for 3s. per day. The *Peacock Hotel* at Baslow has 6½ miles of the Derwent; hotel residents are permitted four rods per day, at a charge of 15s. per rod, wet and dry fly only. The trout season is April 1st to September 30th; grayling June 17th to March 13th. At Rowsley, the *Peacock Hotel* has fishing rights over six miles of the Wye, which abounds in rainbow trout. Fishing is dry fly only, and charges (to hotel residents) are 25*s*. a day. Season for rainbow trout May 16th to November 15th. The hotel also has fishing rights over two miles of the Derwent adjoining the hotel garden, at a charge of 20*s*. per day. For certain stretches of the Lathkil, the Duke of Rutland's Estate Office issues day tickets. The Trent Fishery Board licence must be obtained.

Rock Climbing

Derbyshire with its numerous Gritstone outcrops is becoming increasingly popular for climbers of all degrees of skill. The best of the edges are Stannage, Burbage, Froggatt Curbar, Baslow and Chatsworth, situated on the east side of the upper Derwent valley stretching from Bamford in the north to Chatsworth in the south. The standard of the climbs on these edges ranges from " easy " up to " extremely severe ".

The limestone at Matlock and Dovedale gives excellent practice for artificial climbing, but this is only for the expert and because of the unstable nature of the rock should not be attempted by novices.

Climbing guides for many of the edges are published by the Gritstone Guide Committee and can be bought at most book shops, or from Willmer Bros., 62 Chester Street, Birkenhead.

At White Hall, near Buxton, under the auspices of the Derbyshire County Council, courses on mountaineering and country craft are given by trained instructors.

Speleology

Derbyshire is noted for its caves, many of which have been found in the course of lead mining. Cave explorers and pot-holers have about a hundred caves at their disposal for research and discovery. The main areas are at Castleton (*see* p. 65) and at Matlock (p. 99). There are others in the Manifold Valley (*see* p. 147), at Lathkil, and at Stoney Middleton.

Old Customs

It is perhaps because much of Derbyshire was comparatively isolated for many centuries that various old traditions and customs have survived. The best known is that of *Well Dressing,* which some authorities believe to date from pre-Norman times. It has undoubtedly a religious significance, and at Tissington it may have originated as a thanksgiving when the village escaped the plague of 1340 (the Black Death); it was believed that the pure running water had carried away the infection. Another record shows that the custom was observed in the seventeenth century, when during a long spell of drought—which parched all the surrounding countryside—the five wells of Tissington never ran dry. The custom of well-dressing and well-blessing was revived at Tissington after lapsing during the war years. It is still observed on varying dates throughout the summer in many Derbyshire towns and villages, e.g., Ashford-in-the-Water, Barlow, Bonsall, Bradwell, Buxton, Derby, Eyam, Hope, Stoney Middleton, Tideswell, Tissington, Wirksworth and Youlgreave.

The custom has become an exposition of craftsmanship, bound by tradition and convention. A wooden frame is filled with a foundation of damp clay. On this is traced the outline of a design, generally of a religious character, e.g., the finding of Moses, Jesus appearing to Mary at the well, etc. Into this outline flowers, petals, leaves, seeds and mosses are pressed with great skill to produce an attractive and artistic picture.

Shrovetide has its ancient custom at Ashbourne, where there is the rough and tumble Shrove Tuesday football match, played through the streets of the town.

At Wirksworth, there is a Wakes Sunday, the second in September, when the ceremony of " Clipping the Church " is observed. After a procession through the town, the congregation gathers outside the church and join hands to form a ring; whilst a hymn is sung they slowly circulate round the church.

At Eyam, on the last Sunday in August, a service is held at Cucklet Delf (*see* p. 58) to commemorate the courage and self-sacrifice of the rector and people of Eyam, who during the Plague of 1665 accepted voluntary isolation.

The restoration of Charles II is celebrated as Garland Day or Oakapple Day on May 29th at Castleton. Here a procession headed by the " King " and his " Queen," in seventeenth-century costume, parades the street. The "King" wears a garland, and from this a flower is placed on the war memorial; the rest of the garland is hung on the church tower.

At Alport Barn the Woodlands Lovefeast is held on the first Sunday of July. This custom originated 300 years ago, when people were persecuted for their religious beliefs, and so met in secret to worship. It is attended by a large number of people every year. The following is an extract from Dransfield's *History of Penistone*:—

"At the ejection on Black Bartholomew Day in 1662 when three excellent clergymen in Derby and forty-three in different parts of the country were cast out of their livings and exposed to cruel persecution because each 'Dared to be a Daniel,' at Alport Castles Farm, remote and isolated amid the Derbyshire Moorlands, the Covenanters assembled to worship God according to the dictates of their own consciences, although the sleuth-hounds of persecution were on the scent of the 'Psalm singing rascals' (as they were called) and an implacable soldiery followed them to the inmost recesses of the Peak." In this barn John Wesley preached on several occasions.

At Longshaw sheep-dog trials are held annually at the beginning of September. Dogs are brought from all parts of Great Britain to show their skill and the results of patient training, in rounding up the moorland sheep.

The curfew still "tolls the knell of parting day" in the valleys of Eyam, Castleton and Ashford-in-the-Water; in the Forest chapel of Wildboarclough an annual Rushbearing Service is held in August; and at Chapel-en-le-Frith a " pudding bell " is rung at 11 a.m. each Shrove Tuesday.

BUXTON

General Information

Access and Situation.—Buxton is situated in Derbyshire, in the centre of the Peak District, 159 miles by road from London. Good roads connect it with large centres to north, south, east and west. It is about 20 miles from Ringway airport.

Angling.—*See* p. 16.

Banks.—*Barclays*, 5 The Quadrant; *Midland*, 1 The Quadrant; *Martin's*, 28 Spring Gardens; *District*, 7 Terrace Road and Market Place; *Westminster*, 2 Spring Gardens; *Williams Deacon's*, 1 Cavendish Circus; *Derby Trustee Savings*, 3 The Quadrant.

Bus Services.—Town services radiate from the Market Place. For the surrounding districts there are numerous services—

Macclesfield, viâ Burbage, "Cat and Fiddle," Anchor Lane (for Wildboarclough).
Stockport and Manchester, a convenient route for Peak Dale, Dove Holes, and Chapel-en-le-Frith.
Hayfield and Glossop.
Bakewell, Haddon Hall, Rowsley, Matlock, and Derby.
Hartington and Ashbourne (convenient route for Dovedale).
Leek.
Monsal Head, Baslow and Chesterfield.
Miller's Dale, Tideswell, Eyam and Sheffield.

Car Parks.—(1) Sylvan Park near Railway Viaduct. (2) Hardwick Street, near St. Ann's Well. (3) The Square, near Pavilion. (4) Burlington Road. (5) Water Street. (6) Station Road.

Churches and Chapels

St. John the Baptist (Parish Church): 8, 9.30, 11 and 6.30.
St. Mary's, Dale Road: H.C. at 8, except 2nd Sunday, 9.30 an·
6.30.
St. Anne's, Bath Road: 11 (H.C. at 8 on 2nd Sunday).
Trinity: 11 and 6.30.
St. Peter's, Fairfield: 8, 11 and 6.30.
Christ Church, Burbage: 11 and 6.30.
St. James', Harpur Hill: 11 and 6.30.
Roman Catholic, St. Anne's: 8, 9, 10.30 and 6 or 6.30.
Congregational: Hardwick Mount and Hartington Rd., 11 and 6.30.
Wesleyan: Higher Buxton and London Road, 11 and 6.30.
Methodist: At Burbage and Fairfield, 11 and 6.30.

Clubs and Societies.—Buxton has well-organized Literary, Drama, Music, Photographic and Archaeological Societies. There are various Sports, Motor and Rambling Clubs. The Information Centre will supply details and addresses.

Distances.—*By Road.*—London (*viâ* Matlock), 166, (*viâ* Ashbourne), 161; Derby (*viâ* Matlock), 38, (*viâ* Ashbourne), 33; Birmingham, 79; Sheffield, 29; Leeds, 63; Manchester, 25.

Early Closing Day.—Wednesday, 1 p.m.

Hotels.—*See* p. 10.

Information Bureau.—Office at St. Ann's Well, The Crescent. Telephone BUXTON 114. Maintained jointly by the Corporation and the Peak Park Planning Board.

Library and Museum.—The Public Library and Museum is in Terrace Road. Lending and Reference Library open on weekdays 10–1 and, except on Thursdays, 2.30–7 (Saturdays 5). Reading Room 9.30 a.m. to 9 p.m. The Museum is open 9.30 a.m. to 1 p.m. and 2.30 p.m. to 6 p.m. Saturdays 5 p.m.

At the Library and Museum everything of a fundamental local interest, new or old, is preserved in the Local History Collection. Important archaeological finds, vestiges of the Roman occupation, cave formations, fossils of the local limestone, Blue John and Ashford Marble, pottery, Derbyshire County Maps, local prints, pictures, playbills, photographs and almost 2,000 books and pamphlets dealing with every aspect of local life and activities.

There are also exhibits of old glass, valuable china and a permanent collection of paintings. Temporary exhibitions of loan collections and " one man " art exhibitions are a constant feature.

A special room is set apart for the valuable library bequeathed to the Corporation by Sir William Boyd Dawkins, comprising some 400 volumes of the best known works on archaeology, geology, anthropology and kindred subjects, the five book-cases being from the collection of Louis Napoleon.

Meteorological Instruments and Charts.—On the Slopes there is a Meteorological Station in connection with the Meteorological Office of the Air Ministry. Daily readings and forecasts issued by the Borough Meteorologist are exhibited at the Library and elsewhere. Local time is $7\frac{1}{2}$ minutes later than Greenwich.

Newspaper.—*Buxton Advertiser and Herald*, Fridays.

Population.—19,450.

Postal.—The **Head Post Office** is at the top of the Quadrant. Sub-offices at Higher Buxton, Harpur Hill, Fairfield and Burbage.

Sports and Pastimes

Boating.—Rowing boats and motor boats available on the lake in the Pavilion Gardens.

Bowling.—Greens in Pavilion Gardens, Ashwood Park, Cricket Ground, and Cote Heath Park.

Cricket.—The Park. County cricket matches.

Fishing.—Tickets obtainable from hotels in the vicinity of Wye, Dove, Derwent and Manifold rivers for trout and grayling fishing. For Buxton reservoir, apply to Borough Surveyor, Town Hall. *See* also p. 16.

Football.—Ground at Silverlands.

Golf.—Visitors welcomed as temporary members at *Buxton and High Peak Course*, Fairfield (18 holes) and at the *Cavendish Course* (18 holes) ½-mile west of town centre.

Putting.—Pavilion Gardens and Ashwood Park.

Swimming.—Two pools at the Natural Baths (82° F.), open daily (except Sundays), and at Palace Hotel.

Tennis.—Hard courts in Pavilion Gardens.

Winter Sports.—Tobogganing on the Cresta toboggan run (Cavendish Golf Links) and on the Temple Fields run (College Road).

Entertainments

Carnivals, competitions, and illuminations in Pavilion Gardens.

Children's corner—paddling pool, swings, miniature railway—in Pavilion Gardens.

Cinemas.—*Opera House*, adjoining Pavilion Gardens; *Spa Cinema,* Spring Gardens.

Dancing.—Pavilion Ballroom, and at hotels.

Theatre.—Repertory company at the Playhouse, St. John's Road, Tel. BUXTON 1176.

Well-dressing Festival.—July.

Water Supply.—The water for domestic purposes is obtained from the gritstone watersheds of the hills on the north and west of the town. The capacity of the reservoirs is 117 million gallons. The water is remarkably soft and free from impurities.

Winter Sports.—As soon as snow has fallen and a crisp frost has hardened the roads, everyone begins tobogganing. Those who wish to enjoy the sport under the best conditions proceed to the " Cresta " Toboggan Run on the Cavendish Golf Links, or the Temple Fields Run, at the foot of the woods at the top of College Road.

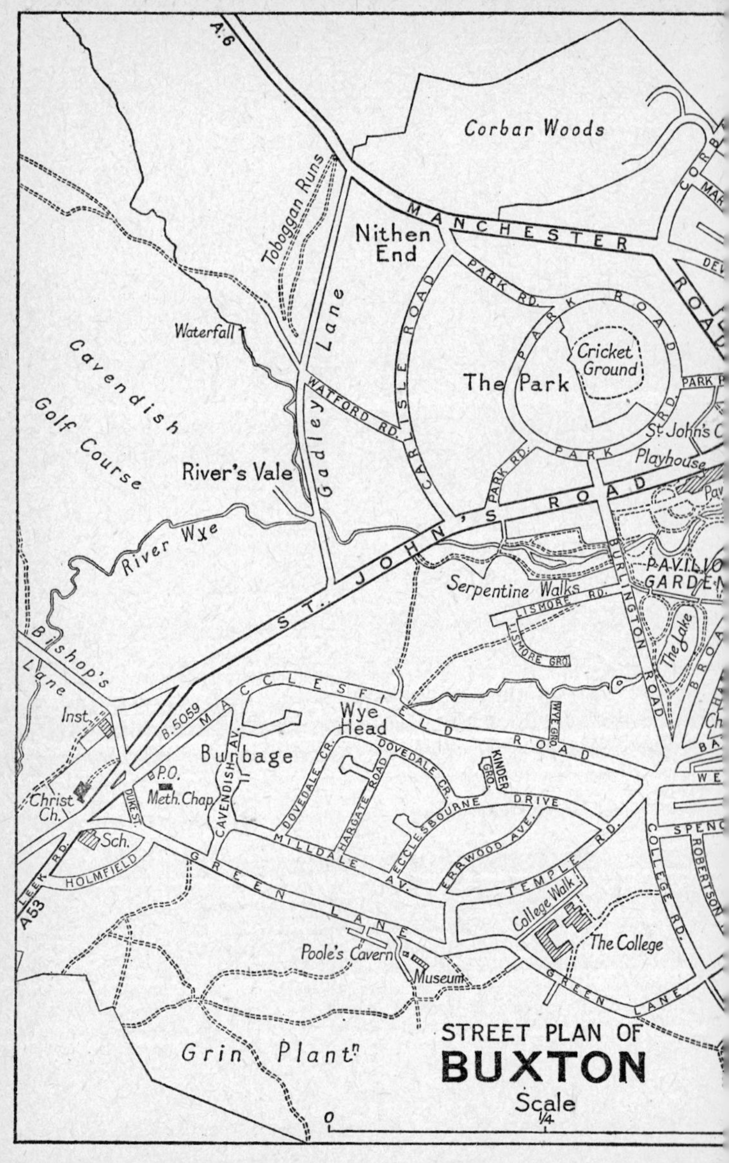

A.6
Corbar Woods
Toboggan Runs
Nithen End
MANCHESTER
ROAD
Waterfall
Cavendish
Golf Course
Gadley Lane
Watford Rd.
Carlisle Road
Park Rd.
PARK ROAD
Cricket Ground
The Park
St. John's C.
Park Rd.
River's Vale
Park Rd.
PARK
ROAD
Playhouse
River Wye
ST. JOHN'S ROAD
Serpentine Walks
Burlington Road
PAVILION GARDEN
The Lake
Lismore Rd.
Lismore Gro.
Bishop's Lane
Inst.
B.5059
MACCLESFIELD
Wye Head
Wye Gro.
BROAD
Burbage
Cavendish Av.
Dovedale Cr.
Dovedale Cr.
Kinder Gro.
ROAD
Ch.
P.O.
Meth. Chap.
Hargate Road
Ecclesbourne
DRIVE
Christ Ch.
Duke St.
Sch.
Milldale Av.
Errwood Av.
College Rd.
Spencer
Robertson
Leek Rd.
Holmfield
Green Lane
Temple Rd.
College Walk
A53
College Walk
The College
Poole's Cavern
Museum
GREEN LANE
Grin Plant^n
STREET PLAN OF
BUXTON
Scale
0
1/4

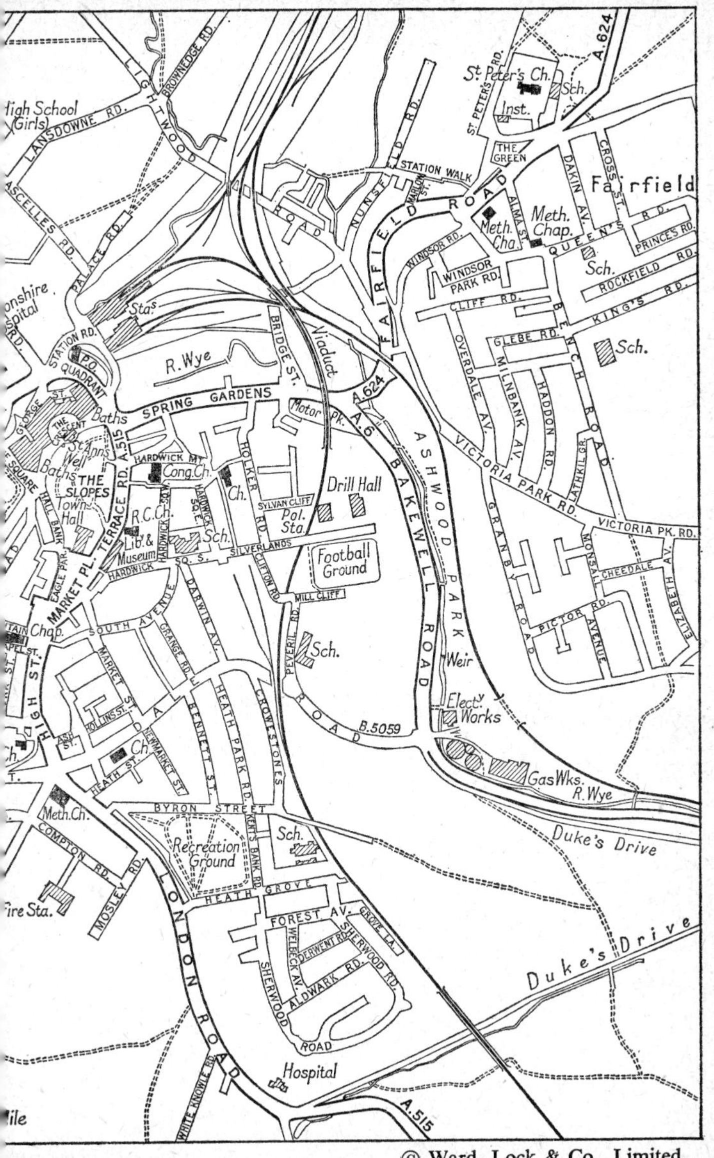

© Ward, Lock & Co., Limited.

IN AND ABOUT BUXTON

Buxton, in the heart of the Peak District, is an attractive holiday and health resort 1,000 feet above sea-level, yet protected by the beautiful surrounding hills. It owes much of its development to the efforts of successive Dukes of Devonshire, whose ancestral home is at Chatsworth, ten miles east of Buxton.

The town is compact and dignified, with gracious buildings, good shops, modern hotels, spacious conference halls, and many acres of parks and public gardens. Its rapid rise to popularity during the last hundred years was largely due to the radio-active thermal springs which have brought relief to thousands of sufferers from rheumatism and allied complaints.

One of these springs is—

St. Ann's Well,

in the centre of the town—at the foot of the terraced walks called the Slopes. This same well was used by the Romans 2,000 years ago, when it may have been dedicated to a pagan goddess. In the Middle Ages, when Buxton was still a mere hamlet, a chapel was built near the well; it was probably about this time that the well was dedicated to St. Ann. For many years sufferers made pilgrimages to St. Ann-of-Buxton, the cured leaving their sticks and crutches near the well, even after the destruction of the chapel in Henry VIII's reign. Among its famous visitors was Mary, Queen of Scots, who, when in the custody of the Earl of Shrewsbury, came several times to take the waters, and was housed in the Old Hall near by. The site of the original house (destroyed in 1670) is now occupied by the *Old Hall Hotel*.

Further growth of Buxton was slow until the opening of a railway from Manchester in 1860. This led to the rapid expansion of the town, and Buxton has now become one of the most popular of inland resorts.

St. Ann's Well is opposite the Crescent. A natural spring of pale blue water wells up into a white marble basin, and yields 200,000 gallons a day. The water is warm (82° F.) and has a pleasant taste. The building covering the well is open daily, and also houses the Information Office; visitors may sit at tables and drink the mineral water at 3d. a glass. The public pump outside the building is supplied by the overflow of the thermal spring.

From the summit of the Slopes, near the well, is an excellent view of the town and its surroundings. Facing the well is the **Crescent:** this colonnaded promenade was built in 1780 on the site of a Roman bath. At the western end of the Crescent the **Natural Baths,** swimming pools supplied by the blue mineral water at a constant temperature of 82° F. from the town's thermal springs. The old Thermal Baths (now closed) are at the eastern wing.

The Buxton waters issue from the limestone rocks at an elevation of 1,000 feet above sea-level at a constant temperature of 82° F. regardless of season. There is a steady flow of 200,000 gallons a day. The water is tasteless and odourless, bright and clear and of a pale blue tint, and remarkably soft to the skin. Since the time of the Romans it has been used as a curative agent in cases of rheumatism, gout, sciatica and neuralgia affections.

The *Old Hall Hotel*, westward of the Natural Baths, occupies the site of a house erected by the Earl of Shrewsbury in the sixteenth century, and pulled down by the Duke of Devonshire in 1670. Mary, Queen of Scots, while in the custody of the Earl of Shrewsbury, was lodged in the original Old Hall during her visits to Buxton for the sake of its healing water, and she is credited with having scratched upon a pane of glass, now preserved in the Museum at Poole's Cavern (p. 30), an adaptation of Caesar's lines upon Feltria. They have been translated—

> " Buxton, whose fame thy milk-warm waters tell,
> Whom I, perhaps, no more shall see, farewell! "

At the back of the *Old Hall Hotel* is the Square, to the left of which are entrances to the Pavilion Gardens, the Opera House and the Union Club. Up the hill is the Devonshire Royal Hospital, and another road leads to the chief **Post Office.**

In our bird's-eye view of the town a huge dome and two small domes and a clock tower lying behind the Crescent mark the position of—

The Devonshire Royal Hospital

The Hospital was opened in 1859 for the treatment of patients suffering from rheumatism and allied diseases. During the Cotton Famine 100 destitute female operatives were received into the Hospital; and when the governors of the Cotton Districts Convalescent Fund divided the balance left in their hands after the famine was over, they handed to the authorities a sum of £24,000 to enable them to extend and improve the buildings. In 1914 was erected a new mineral-water bathing establishment. In 1921 H.R.H. the Princess Royal (then Princess Mary) laid the commemoration stone of a new wing, containing dining-rooms for patients and staff, and also stores and kitchen. The Hospital was taken over by the Minister of Health in July 1948 under the provisions of the National Health Service Act, 1946.

The great dome is the largest of its kind in the world, its diameter being 156 feet. The area covered by it is half an acre, sufficient to hold 6,000 persons. Nearly the whole of the space, 1,000,000 cubic feet, is available to the patients for exercise and amusement, thus rendering them independent of the weather. Immediately under the lantern of the dome a very remarkable echo may be heard.

The hospital is now devoted to the treatment of long-term in-patients. All modern forms of hydrotherapy, physiotherapy and occupational therapy are available and over 100,000 treatments are given annually.

The trees and ground behind the Hospital as we look on it from the Slopes are—

The Corbar Crags and Wood

threaded by numerous paths of easy gradients that wind through plantations and traverse the picturesque inequalities of old quarries, covered with trees, shrubs, ferns and wild flowers, and afford charming views of the town and the surrounding hills. The entrance to the walks is about half a mile from the Crescent and reached by passing through the iron turnstile on the right of Manchester Road. The return walk may be varied by bearing right to Corbar Road, then left along Marlborough Road.

The district immediately below Manchester Road is **The Park.** Here are many charming residences, and in the centre is a well-kept **Cricket and Bowling Ground,** with a pavilion. County Cricket matches are played here.

Westward of the Park, and between St. John's Road and Manchester Road, is the **Cavendish Golf Course.**

Close to the foot of the Slopes and adjoining the Devonshire Hospital is a cupola-crowned building, the **Parish Church of St. John the Baptist,** with some good nineteenth-century mosaics and glass. It was built in 1811 as the completion of the fifth Duke of Devonshire's plans for developing Buxton. Extensive alterations were made in 1898.

To the left of St. John's Church and nearer our view-point is the **Opera House,** used mainly as a cinema.

The adjoining **Pavilion** can accommodate 2,000 people. It is administered by Buxton Corporation and comprises a well-maintained Concert Hall and Ballroom, a theatre, **The Playhouse,** and restaurant and cafeteria. There are pleasant sun-lounges overlooking—

The Pavilion Gardens

(Admission, 1s.; Children, 6d.)

These cover 23 acres of artistically laid out grounds, through which the River Wye meanders and cascades. There are smooth lawns and shady walks. Ample facilities are provided for tennis, bowls and putting, and for the children there is a miniature railway, a playground and a paddling pool.

To the west of the gardens the Wye flows between pleasantly wooded banks, forming a kind of extension of the Gardens, known as the **Serpentine Walks.** Here are shady paths and riverside seats.

From the southern end beyond the boating lake, Burlington Road and Temple Road lead to—

Poole's Cavern

(**Admission,.** 1*s*. 6*d*. **Open** daily, 1st April to 31st October.)

This is a large cave in a hill called **Grin Low,** three-quarters of a mile from the Crescent. It is said to be named after an outlaw who lived in the reign of Henry IV: but he was not its first inhabitant, for even in prehistoric times the cavern was a human residence, as was demonstrated by the discovery of the kitchen-midden, or refuse food heap, of the primitive cave-dwellers. Under a stalagmite floor, Roman articles of pottery, jewellery and tools have been found.

Outside the cavern is a **Museum,** with a miscellaneous assortment of objects, including relics of early ages, some engravings and paintings, a " Treacle " Bible, a " Breeches " Bible (*see* also p. 67), a copy of Cotton's *Wonders of the Peak*, furniture, a copy of the *Plain Man's Path to Heaven*, from which John Bunyan is said to have derived the idea of his immortal work; and the pane of glass referred to on p. 27.

The cavern extends for about half a mile and is well lighted. The roofings and arches are of imposing extent and character, the loftiest chamber being 90 feet high. There are numerous stalactites and stalagmites. Some of these are exceptionally fine, and have been given more or less fanciful names, such as the Flitch of Bacon, the Chair, the Font, the Lion, etc. There is also Mary, Queen of Scots' Pillar, so called because that unfortunate queen is said to have leant against it.

The Wye enters the cavern soon after leaving its head springs.

Breaking the eastern skyline as we continue our survey of Buxton from above St. Ann's Well is the tower of the parish church of—

Fairfield

approached by a steep ascent, presenting on the left a good view of the whole valley of Buxton, backed by Grin Low, Axe Edge, Burbage Edge and Black Edge, while Lower Buxton and the adjacent park occupy the centre of the scene.

Beyond Fairfield lies an extensive **Common**—once the Buxton Race-course. On the Common—or the *Barms* as the tract is locally called—are the **Golf Links** and club-house of the Buxton and High Peak Golf Club.

Fairfield Church is dedicated to St. Peter. It was built in 1839, on the site of a chapel dating from the time of Queen Elizabeth. A memorial table within attracts attention by the singular motto of the Dakin family: " Strike, Dakin; the Devil's in the Hemp."

The silver chalice in use in the Church is dated 1595. In the churchyard is a sundial on a pedestal which is believed to be a fragment of an ancient cross.

Now from our vantage-point on St. Ann's Cliff we may turn about. The building at the top of the hill and immediately in front of us is—

The Town Hall

containing the Council Chamber and Municipal Offices. The principal front of the Hall faces the Market Place in Higher Buxton, the terminus of most of the bus services. In the square is the restored **Market Cross** of the town.

On the south side of the Market Place starts the **High Street.** Towards the farther end this thoroughfare narrows, and to the right, at the point where the broader portion ceases, is the approach to—

St. Anne's Church

This Anglican place of worship is, with the exception of the Old Hall (now used as an hotel), the oldest public building in the town. It is a small, primitive building, erected in 1625, and is the direct descendant of the " Well-chapel " which stood on the site of the present Old Hall. At the Reformation both the chapel and the statue of the patron saint with which it was ornamented fell victims to the iconoclastic zeal of the times. For nearly a hundred years Buxton was without a church, and when the present edifice was erected it was dedicated to St. John, in order to counteract the veneration which was attached to the saint to whose influence the medicinal virtues of the waters were attributed. But it was only known by its new name for a short time, and the convenience of its original one became apparent on the restoration of the Church. St. Anne's has a stone-slabbed roof, supported by stout tie-beams, and a bell-turret, unusual for these parts. The font is Jacobean and oblong in shape, and there is a carved seventeenth-century oak reading-desk.

The general line of the High Street is continued by the **London Road,** which about half a mile south of Higher Buxton is joined by the **Duke's Drive** (*see* below). To the right of this, at the foot of Harpur Hill Road, is *Sherbrook Lodge*, the Buxton Youth Hostel.

From the bottom of the Slopes **Spring Gardens** run eastward. This is Buxton's principal business thoroughfare. At the far end, below the lofty railway viaduct, is a large **Car Park;** just beyond the viaduct the road forks: to the left is the way to Fairfield (*see* p. 30), Chapel-en-le-Frith, Castleton, and the Hope Valley; the right-hand road is that for Bakewell and Matlock. Eastward from the Slopes the valley of the Wye runs parallel to Spring Gardens and the railway through Ashwood Park and—

Ashwood Dale

a charming valley. The rocks which form the sides of the valley are very varied; some bare and sombre, others tree-covered, others clad with ivy, ferns, and evergreens. At the Buxton end of the valley is **Ashwood Park,** with bowling greens (Crown type), tennis courts, putting green, walks and gardens, and a children's corner.

A few hundred yards from the viaduct the Dale bears to the left and on the right is the entrance to **Sherbrook Dell,** a beautiful nook. Here is the *Lovers' Leap,* a huge natural cleft in the limestone rock rising steeply from Ashwood Dale, of which it commands a splendid view. The ascent from the other side is more gradual. The name is traditionally traced to a desperate leap of two runaway lovers riding one horse, who by that means evaded the pursuit of the lady's parents.

The upper end of Sherbrook Dell adjoins the road known as the **Duke's Drive.** It was constructed in 1795 by the then Duke of Devonshire. The Drive may be entered either at the corner by the Gas Works or near the Hospital on the London Road at Higher Buxton. The circuit (nearly 3 miles) makes a pleasant round giving good views.

Buxton from the Town Hall (*J. Salmon*)

Serpentine Walks, Pavilion Gardens, Buxton (*J. Salmon*)

Chee Dale (*J. Salmon*)

Monsal Dale (*J. Salmon*)

WALKS AROUND BUXTON

Some of the most beautiful scenery in the vicinity of Buxton can be visited only by walkers. Footpaths afford the only access to many of the Derbyshire dales, and the finest bits of moorland lie off the high road.

I.—GADLEY LANE AND WATFORD WOOD

Go along Manchester Road behind the Devonshire Hospital to the Cavendish Golf Course. Descend the lane passing the Club House, cross a footbridge, then the stile on the left. The path leads to the Serpentine Walks (*see* p. 29) and, by turning left, the town centre is reached (2 *miles*).

To prolong the above walk (*to 4 miles*) follow the cart track across the Cavendish Golf Course to *Watford Farm*. Go round the back of the farm *viâ* a small gate and ascend the woods to the next farm. From here a rough track leads to a road which meets St. John's Road, where turn left to gain the town centre.

II.—TO GRIN LOW TOWER

The conspicuous round tower which crowns the summit of **Grin Low,** the hill containing Poole's Cavern, replaces an older tower which was known as Solomon's Temple. The name of the hill was originally borne by a barrow which served as the foundation of the temple. The barrow, when opened in 1894, was found to contain the remains of six bodies, flint flakes and fragments of pottery. The tower was erected in 1896 on the site of the former structure, built to afford employment to a number of men then out of work, on land occupied by a good-natured and well-to-do farmer, Solomon Mycock by name. Standing as it does about 1,440 feet above sea-level, it commands a very extensive view, including Black Edge (beyond Buxton) with Kinder Scout to the right of it, Rushup Edge and the distinctive Mam Tor, the Peak Forest moorlands, the winding Wye Valley (to the east), the much-quarried Harpur Hill and Hind Low, and the long ridges of Axe Edge and Burbage Edge to the west.

The tower is approached by a footpath which leaves Green Lane exactly opposite College Road, a thoroughfare running south from Broad Walk; another path begins near the entrance to Poole's Cavern (p. 29) and ascends through Grin Low Woods; the two combined make a pleasant circular walk of about 2½ miles.

Visitors who desire to extend their walk may follow Green Lane westward to **Burbage** (½-mile), from which the return may be made by bus. Or the walk may be still further prolonged by returning to Buxton *via* Macclesfield Road or St. John's Road.

III.—TO COWDALE

Cowdale is the bourne of a pleasant walk along a bridle-path leading to the left from the Duke's Drive (*see* p. 32) to **Staden,** and thence across fields to **Cowdale,** about 2½ miles from Buxton. A lane descends from here for a quarter of a mile to the Bakewell road (along which the buses run), opposite Pic Tor, about 2 miles from Buxton.

IV.—TO KING STERNDALE

By continuing eastward along the dale for another mile a steep, rough road is reached leading to the hamlet of **King Sterndale.** There is a picturesque green and the remains of an ancient cross (recently restored), but the church is a modern building.

V.—TO AXE EDGE

From its height and commanding position, **Axe Edge** provides a favourite excursion from the town. The summit is more than 1,800 feet above sea-level, and the high road along its eastern flank reaches an altitude of over 1,600 feet; but, as the lowest part of Buxton is about 1,000 feet high, the eminence does not seem so lofty as it really is.

The road (A53) to Axe Edge, along which the Leek buses

pass, lies through Burbage, keeping to the left where the road forks just past the Church, and again to the left half a mile farther on. In a little over two miles a green cart-track strikes up to the right and may be followed over the Edge to the *Cat and Fiddle* road 1½ miles above Burbage and on the Macclesfield bus route. Another rough road, taking approximately the same direction, turns off three-quarters of a mile farther along the Leek road.

Or the walk may be extended to **Flash** (*see* p. 48), or alternatively one may search for the sources of the *Dove* and the *Manifold*. The former lies to the left of the road just under four miles from Buxton. Opposite **Dove Head Farm** a flagged path leads down to the probable source of the river. On the capstone covering the spring are carved the initials of Isaak Walton and Charles Cotton, to whom the Dove owes so much of its fame.

The *Manifold* rises a quarter of a mile farther on, behind the *Traveller's Rest Inn*. The walk may be continued from the Inn to **Panniers Pool Bridge, Three Shires Head** (p. 37) (here Derbyshire, Cheshire and Staffordshire meet), and to the head of the Dane, which lies near the Congleton road, and thence to the *Cat and Fiddle Inn* (*see* below).

VI.—TO THE "CAT AND FIDDLE"

Leave Buxton by the Burbage road. At the War Memorial the main Macclesfield road keeps straight on, turning to the right by A537 about half a mile farther. Walkers, however, are recommended to bear to the right at the War Memorial and to use the old coach road. The two roads approach each other just above a reservoir, then they separate until finally they meet short of the Inn, which is 4 miles

from Buxton by the Old Road, nearly 5 miles by the main road.

The *Cat and Fiddle Inn*, at the highest point on the Macclesfield road, is 1,690 feet above sea-level, and consequently the house is, next to that at Tan Hill, in the North Riding of

Yorkshire (1,727 feet), the most loftily situated hostelry in England. The view westward from the Inn over the Cheshire Plain is remarkably fine, the most striking features being the Mersey and the giant telescope at Jodrell Bank, which are clearly visible.

The peculiar sign of the Inn has given rise to a good deal of discussion. According to one absurd story, a certain Duke of Devonshire was accustomed to drive up the ascent to the house, and to take with him a favourite cat and fiddle. Dr. Brewer, in his *Phrase and Fable*, after glancing at another alleged origin—a corruption of " Caton Fidele," i.e. " Caton, the Faithful," governor of Calais, adds:—" Without scanning the phrase so nicely, it may simply mean the game of ' cat ' (trap-ball) and a fiddle for dancing provided for customers." Possibly a much simpler origin is in the well-known nursery rhyme.

Buxton may be regained by bus, or by the Old Road: of the various alternatives we will mention two:—

(*a*) Follow the main road back for about a mile and then take the track on the right over the Axe Edge, descending to the Leek road (4½ miles to Buxton).
(*b*) Where the road bends to the left near the *Cat and Fiddle* there is a stile on the right leading to a path across the moor passing Shining Tor and the Erwood Estate. Continue along the track to the Goyt valley, cross the old packhorse bridge and bear right at the long hill to the Manchester road and Burbage.

VII.—TO WILDBOARCLOUGH

As the crow flies, Wildboarclough lies about 6 miles south-west of Buxton, but the walk is considerably longer. The Macclesfield bus, however, may be used at the beginning and end of the route, and there are buses (on weekdays only) from the Macclesfield road to Wildboarclough itself.

Proceed by the Congleton road (A54) nearly to the sixth milestone, then turn to the right, dropping downhill between trees and forking to the left in just over a quarter of a mile into **Wildboarclough,** the soft beauty of which is enhanced by comparison with the bleak scenes around. Carpet works established during the last century were a failure, and the place now consists only of the church, the post office, and a few residences. The name arose from the tradition that here was killed the last wild boar in England.

The road to the right from the church ascends a quietly beautiful valley, overlooked by Shutlings Low, a hill reminiscent of Ingleborough, to the *Stanley Arms Inn*, about 9 miles out from Buxton (buses). Hence we climb to the right for about 1½ miles to the *Cat and Fiddle*, "and so home."

VIII.—TO PANNIERS POOL BRIDGE

Follow the road over Axe Edge (p. 34) or take the Leek bus, alighting about 150 yards short of the *Traveller's Rest Inn*. Turn off to the right here and descend by a rough road. Join another, coming in on the right, go left at a junction, and at the next junction, turn up to the right. Before reaching Knotbury Farm bear left into a green cart-track, which descends to cross a charming little brook coming down from Axe Edge. Go to the left, and in a short distance **Panniers Pool Bridge** will be found, spanning the Dane. The distance from the *Traveller's Rest* is nearly 2 miles.

At the junction of the two streams, the three counties of Derbyshire, Cheshire and Staffordshire meet, and from this circumstance the spot is frequently alluded to as **Three Shires Head.** The bridge and mountain torrent, set against a background of heather, gorse, and bracken, form a charming picture.

The simplest continuation of the walk is to follow the Dane downstream on its right bank to the Flash–Allgreave road at Midgleygate, which is quite close to Manor Farm and the lane leading to Gradbach Mill and Ludchurch (*see* p. 49).

Another, perhaps better, route is to ascend by a track which goes first alongside the Dane upstream and then winds up to the farm of Holt, below the Congleton road. Turn right along the road towards Buxton: there is a grand view of Axe Edge and towards the Roaches. At the top of the hill, above a derelict mine, take a track on to the moor to the left. This leads to the *Cat and Fiddle Inn* (p. 35), about 3 miles from Panniers Pool Bridge. Near its highest point it is joined by a track which comes up from Wildboarclough by the Cumberland Brook.

IX.—TO THE GOYT VALLEY AND JENKIN CHAPEL

Climb the ascending Manchester road for nearly two miles to the top of Long Hill, whence a rugged mountain road on the left leads downhill to **Goyt's Bridge.** From the bridge the Goyt may be traced nearly to its source by going along the road to the left and following the footpath which crosses the river one and a half miles from the Bridge and finally rejoins the old coach road three-quarters of a mile from Burbage. This footpath route becomes very slippery in wet weather, when it is advisable to keep to the road alongside the Goyt, which meets the old coach road from Macclesfield. The distance for the complete round is about 8½ miles.

It is a very pleasant walk northward from the bridge along the western side of the newly-formed lake to Taxal and Whaley Bridge (about 4 miles), whence Buxton can be regained by bus; or by crossing the suspension bridge near the southern end of the reservoir a way can be made to the Manchester-Buxton road between Fernilee and Whaley Bridge, just over 5 miles from Buxton. (Buses from Horwich End, about a mile farther on.)

The narrow road climbing to the right, out of the valley, from Goyt's Bridge is known as **The Street,** being in fact a Roman road. Near the top of the hill the road turns right for Kettleshulme—buses to Macclesfield and Whaley Bridge— and we continue straight and down hill, and in less than a mile reach **Jenkin Chapel,** a barn-like building in a lonely spot. A notice over the west door states " St. John the Baptist Free Chapel was June 24/1733 erected." Stout stone steps outside the chapel lead to a gallery, and, inside, the chapel retains its " horse-box " pews and three-decker pulpit. A further architectural " curiosity " is the shape and size of the windows, which are not at all what one would expect to find in a chapel.

Turn to the left at the chapel, and follow the narrow road as it winds and steeply rises and falls. (The hairpin bend known as *The Winkle* is famous in motor trials.) Finally, the Macclesfield road (bus route) is reached about 8¼ miles from Buxton and some 2½ miles from the *Cat and Fiddle.*

X.—TO COMBS LAKE AND CHAPEL-EN-LE-FRITH

A delightful walk of about 6 miles. The bus can be used for the return from Chapel-en-le-Frith. The lake, or rather reservoir, is northward of Buxton, and the route lies along the Long Hill road for about a mile, then along a lane on the right which passes over the moor. Near White Hall a path across a field to the right leads into a steep lane that goes down into the pretty hamlet of **Combs,** a short distance beyond which, reached by the road to the right of the *Bee Hive Inn*, is the lake, picturesquely situated among the hills.

The scene is most impressive soon after a storm, while the water, looking like white ribbons on the black rocks, is rushing down the dark gritstone cliffs which form the edge of Combs Moss.

The lane leads into the Stockport road less than a mile to the west of—

Chapel-en-le-Frith

an old market town once "the chapel in the forest." The derivation of the name is obvious when we remember that this district was a royal forest. The **Church** was first built in 1225 by the keepers of the forest, who dedicated it to St. Thomas Becket. Some traces of the original chapel remain in the chancel walls. The nave is probably late fourteenth-century and the font is fifteenth-century. In 1733 a new tower was built and the south side of the church refaced in the classical style of that time. The old part of Chapel-en-le-Frith consists mainly of one long street and about fifteen scattered hamlets, some of which are very picturesque. There are old inns, stocks and a market cross.

XI.—KINDER SCOUT

Kinder Scout, an area measuring approximately five miles in length and $2\frac{1}{2}$ miles in width at the widest part to two hundred yards at the narrowest, reaches a maximum altitude of 2,088 feet. It is part of the plateau called the "Peak," a strictly preserved grouse moor, north of Buxton, which until 1954 was officially closed to the public, although permission to use one path had been secured in 1897 by the efforts of the Peak District and Northern Counties Footpaths Preservation Society.

The route of roughly 12 miles runs from **Jacob's Ladder**, a steep track at the western end of Edale, to the *Snake Inn* on the road between Glossop and Sheffield; but since the whole course is for strong walkers only it is more conveniently regarded as being in two sections. The first is entered from Edale by following the road to the westward from Edale through Barber Booth and Upper Booth to Edale Head; thence by the rough lane of Jacob's Ladder indicated by a signpost erected by the Peak District and Footpath Society. This is the old pack-horse way and leads to the shaft of Edale Cross, scarcely visible behind the wall on the right at its highest point and down to the reservoir at the foot of William Clough, north-east of Hayfield, with good views of the western flank of Kinder and of the famous Downfall. The route is well indicated. Those making for Hayfield will find a more direct track on the left soon after passing Edale Cross—the *Coldwell Clough* route.

Arrangements have now been completed with several landowners allowing access by the public to a large slice of the Kinder plateau, formerly officially closed. In the north, the access land or open country includes Ashop Head, Fairbrook Naze, Seal Edge and Blackden Edge and extends to Crookstone Moor in the east where the Roman Road and the right of way up Jagger's Clough lead to the access land. Southwards the area includes Rowland Cote Moor, Golden Clough, Grindsbrook, Edale Moor and Crowden Head, with such well-known features as Crowden Tower, Pym Chair, the Wool Packs, Jacob's Ladder and Edale Cross. In the west the area is bounded by Mount Famine and South Head and includes Kinderlow End and the famous "Downfall." The moorlands to which the public have been given general access under these agreements will, however, be closed to visitors each year on 12th August, and every subsequent Monday during August and September, for shooting.

Hayfield, about 7 miles westward from Edale, is a small town occupying a site some 650 feet above sea-level, at the western foot of Kinder Scout. It is connected with both Manchester and Buxton by rail or bus and so is a popular starting point for Kinder Scout. The houses are built of stone, and on the whole the town wears a bleak appearance. Indeed, a proverb tells us that " the neighbourhood of Kinder Scout is the coldest place that's out."

Hayfield to the Snake Pass.—Leave the main street of Hayfield by the passage which starts on the left (north) side of the *Royal Hotel* and leads into a cobbled road. This road becomes a bridle-road, bearing round to the left and bringing one with the minimum of exertion to the reservoir at the foot of William Clough. The Snake path (signposted) goes to the left of the reservoir, along the flank of the hillside running down to the water. Those who ascend by the hill path from Hayfield soon have a good view of the valley of the *Sett*, with New Mills and the hills about Disley. After passing the last of the gates the moorland is uninterrupted. In little more than a mile from Hayfield another track joins the one we are on. About a quarter of a mile from the junction take a path to the left, leaving the bridle-road. From this point a distant view is obtained of the **Downfall,** a cataract which descends from the highest ridge in successive plunges. The water is of no great volume except after heavy rain; although when blown into spray by stormy winds it often extends to a width of a quarter of a mile. It is the biggest thing in waterfalls in the neighbourhood of Manchester, and H. B. Biden considered that Kinder Scout itself owes its name to the Fall, the words " Kin-" (or " cin ") " dwr-Scwd," of which that name is a corruption, meaning " the high-water cataract." Below the foot of the fall is a lonely tarn known as the **Mermaid's Pool,** concerning which the natives tell many wonderful stories.

From the point at which the distant view of the Downfall is obtained, proceed along the hillside, with the reservoir on the right, to Nab Brow, when the path drops down to the sheepfold in **William Clough,** over 1,000 feet above sea-level. The path now follows the brook course. Still rising, we pass on the right the third mile-post from Hayfield and arrive at the foot of **Mill Hill** (1,761 feet). The ascent is steep and the moors so boggy that it is dangerous to stray from the path.

There is small chance of going astray—except in mist or darkness—for the path is well worn and there are numerous marking posts. From Mill Hill the direction is eastward down the left bank of the *Ashop* to its confluence with the Lady Clough Brook, over which is a footbridge. The main road is only a hundred yards or so distant. Turn right along the main road and the *Snake Inn* will be seen on the left. From the *Snake* the approximate distance to Glossop is 7 miles; Bamford 10; Hope, *viâ* the Roman Road, 8; Edale, by the same road and Jagger's Clough, 7½. Return to Buxton from Bamford, Hope or Edale, or from Glossop may be made by bus.

Hayfield to Edale.—Leave by the cobbled road mentioned above. If time permits, follow this to the waterworks, at the entrance to which cross the stream. The lane ascends and bears round to the right, and soon there appears on the right a path which leads behind a small plantation and then turns up to the right and in due course comes to Edale Cross. The shorter but steeper route leaves the cobbled road at a bridge over the river less than a mile from Hayfield. The route follows the *River Sett* towards its source for ¾-mile and then bears up to the left through **Coldwell Clough** and so to Edale Cross.

From the Cross descend into Edale by Jacob's Ladder or the easier alternative, and follow a lane through Upper Booth to the hamlet of Barber Booth. The road to the left here is that for Edale (about a mile); that to the right climbs to *Mam Nick*, on the far side of which is the Castleton–Chapel-en-le-Frith road; but good walkers are recommended to take, in preference to either road from Barber Booth, the track striking up on the right 200 yards short of the junction-roads. This climbs to **Rushup Edge.** Here is a tumulus known as *Lord's Seat* which with several acres of adjoining land has been acquired by the National Trust. There is a splendid walk along Rushup Edge to Mam Nick (*see* p. 74).

XII.—THROUGH THE VALE OF EDALE

The route from Hayfield to Edale has already been described above. The following route is a little shorter and is hardly less interesting. The path starts from the highest point of the main road between Chapel-en-le-Frith and Hayfield. (The Buxton–Glossop buses pass this point.) About 150 yards beyond a road up from Chinley a lane strikes off to the right through ground where there is a quarry. This leads into a long lane, the old road from Hayfield to the Castleton road. A few yards up this lane is one of the Peak District Society's direction indicators. Cross the field to the next gate, known locally as Gee's banks, whence a view is gained of the whole of the Kinder Valley, with the encircling hills and the Scout. **Coldwell Clough** and the Edale track are right in front. Up the latter in clear weather may be seen a white speck; this is the Society's plate at Stonyford stile. At the bridge over the Sett the four or five paths which cross the Kinder Valley join the Edale road. Turn to the right up the lane, past the farmhouse, opposite which is a sun-dial (17 | E.B. | 06). Beyond this farmyard one of the field-paths from the lower part of the valley joins our track. A few hundreds yards farther, at the gate on the left, the bridle road from the Glossop road over **Leygate Moor** joins the Edale road. Presently the Stonyford guide-plate is in sight, and then the summit of the road is reached, with **Edale Cross** (p. 42) on the left behind the wall. Shortly on the left, Edale rocks and the Noe Stool are seen in the distance. Coming to the bottom of a bit of rough path, the road takes a sudden turn to the right across the face of the hill. At this turn, on the left, is a step-stile which leads down to what is known as *Jacob's Ladder*, rejoining the track at the brook below. A few fields farther the route passes through the yard of Lee House, and shortly crosses the *Crowden Brook* to Upper Booth.

There are now two alternatives:—

(*a*) Down to the right is the cart-road—rather roundabout.

(*b*) Turn to left into the farmyard. Behind the house on the right is the beginning of a field-path which rejoins the road at **Barber Booth.**

The road continues down the valley to join that from **Edale** village (p. 63).

If it is desired to visit Castleton by way of Mam Tor and the Winnats, turn to the right over the bridge before arriving at the Edale road, then follow the side of a little rift and ascend thence to the road over Mam Nick (p. 74). If another route is preferred, enter a path before coming to the old churchyard on the left, cross over a bridge, and, passing through the first gateway, take a field-path which strikes off to the right and leads down to the bridge over the *River Noe*. The path crosses the bridge, then rises by Hollins Farm to the crest of the hill at Hollins Cross, about a mile and a half from Castleton (p. 65). If it is not desired to visit Castleton, keep along the ridge-top to Lose Hill and descend thence by a distinctive path to Hope (p. 64).

The road through the Vale of Edale to Hope is quietly pleasant, if lacking something of the excitement of the hilly tracks on either hand. Above Nether Booth, on the southern slopes of Edale Moor, is the finely-situated Youth Hostel of Rowland Cote. Nearly 3 miles east of Edale village is the beginning of a fine route over to the Derwent Reservoirs and the Woodlands Valley by way of Jagger's Clough; or from the summit of the climb above the clough, where is *Hope Cross*, one may strike along the ridge and gain Thornhill or Bamford by way of Win Hill (*see* p. 64). The Jagger's Clough route may also be used in conjunction with the William Clough route (p. 41) to make the circuit of the High Peak.

XIII.—TO RUSHUP EDGE AND MAM TOR

The finest ridge walk in the district begins about 3 miles from Chapel-en-le-Frith on the Castleton road. Here a path goes off on the left and shortly comes out on **Rushup Edge,** from which there are grand views; in one direction over the Edale Valley to the Kinder Scout plateau; in the other to the moors of Peak Forest and to Black Edge and Axe Edge. When the Edge ends at Mam Nick, cross the road, climb Mam Tor (p. 64) and continue along the grassy ridge dividing the Edale and Hope Valleys to Lose Hill, whence a descent is made to Hope (9 miles from Chapel).

XIV.—TO CHEE DALE AND MILLER'S DALE

The Bakewell buses run past the entrance to Chee Dale and the Tideswell buses serve Miller's Dale.

It should be noted that much of the path is rough and " scrambly " and even dangerous after rain to all but the sure-footed. At least 1½ hours should be allowed for the walk from the foot of Deep Dale to Miller's Dale.

Follow the Bakewell road along Ashwood Dale (*see* p. 32) for just over 3 miles, or travel by bus as far as **Topley Pike,** then opposite the entrance to Deep Dale (to the right) take a bridle path to the left which goes through the woods near the *Wye.* Cross the river by a footbridge, opposite the foot of Great Rocks Dale, turn to the right, then keep on alongside the river. The path leads through the lovely **Chee Dale,** which is of horseshoe shape and forms one of the best bits of limestone scenery in the country. On the south side is **Chee Tor,** a magnificent crag, almost cylindrical. It is upwards of 300 feet high, but its perpendicular sides cause the altitude to appear greater; they are as straight as if cleft by the hand of man.

The going is rather rough, particularly through the narrowest part of the dale.

Beyond the Tor the path crosses an interesting little stream near the point where it comes to the surface after travelling underground from Wormhill. The path issues into the Tideswell road, a good 6 miles from Buxton by this route.

Miller's Dale forms the next part of the valley of the Wye and extends eastward from the hamlet of the same name. On the left is the *Railway Hotel* and, opposite, an old corn mill now modernised. Continue eastward along the road to Miller's Dale church where the road forks, to the right for the *Angler's Rest Inn* and Litton Mill and to the left for Tideswell. The old road facing the red telephone box also leads to Tideswell. At **Litton Mill** the water of the Wye is pent up by a weir. Many visitors turn back at this point, but it is a very delightful walk on to **Cressbrook,** from which the return to Buxton can be made. The lane from Litton Mill to Cressbrook is private, but pedestrians are allowed to use it. It is a little-used lane running close beside the river with charming views of trees and rocks. The Dale is a haunt of the kingfisher.

On emerging into the road at Cressbrook turn to the right. A lane, crossing the river about half a mile farther on, ascends to the head of Monsal Dale, about $9\frac{1}{2}$ miles from Buxton. Those who thirst for more of this lovely scenery, however, may extend the walk by following the river down through **Monsal Dale** (*see* p. 79) to the main road (bus route) at the foot of Taddington Dale (about $1\frac{1}{2}$ miles more). Or a charming walk may be taken through the thickly wooded **Cressbrook Dale** and across fields to Litton and Tideswell (about 5 miles from Miller's Dale by this route), whence there are buses to Buxton.

XV.—TO DEEPDALE

The entrance to Deepdale is on the right of the Bakewell road at the foot of the buttress-like cliff of Topley Pike, just over 3 miles from Buxton. From the highway it might be mistaken for a quarry, but actually Deepdale is a typical dry limestone valley, a mile and a half long. Rain and frost have splintered off pieces of rock, and these, slipping down the steep sides, have formed immense screes. The limestone cliffs resemble the bastions of an old-world fortress. They are tenanted by flocks of jackdaws, and are pierced by innumerable caves.

Deepdale Cavern, in the upper portion of the valley, is about 100 yards long. It has yielded human bones, tools, skeletons of animals, pottery, wooden weapons, and so forth. The collection of relics of the Romano-British period obtained from it was said by Boyd-Dawkins to be the largest of the kind found in any similar cave. Some of the relics may be seen in the Buxton Museum.

Deepdale and its rightward continuation, **Back Dale,** communicate with the Ashbourne road near Brierlow Bar Farm, about 3 miles south-east of Buxton (buses). Or Chelmorton can be included in the excursion, and the return made by the Bakewell-Buxton bus.

If the latter course is adopted, leave Deepdale about 100 yards north of the Cavern, cross a stile and a stone bridge, walk up a zigzag and pass a smaller cave. Then follow the footpath, the grass lane, and the road to Chelmorton, about 6 miles from Buxton by this route.

XVI.—CHELMORTON

Chelmorton is the highest village in the county, a bench mark on the church giving a height of 1,209 feet above sea-level. It is best reached from Buxton by way of Brierlow Bar, on the Ashbourne road about 3 miles out from Buxton (buses), then turning left and walking eastward for about 2 miles. Formerly a little stream ran down the village street, but is now piped underground and is no longer seen. At one time the place was a centre of busy lead mining activity.

The **Church** is in the Decorated and Perpendicular styles. An unusual feature of the interior is a fourteenth-century stone rood-screen, five to six feet high, with traceried panels. There are also a fifteenth-century stone font, three piscinae and two sedilia, the seats formed of an incised slab. In the churchyard is a very old stone cross. The church was carefully restored in 1874, the ancient stone coffin slabs then unearthed are now in the porch. Its bells (oldest 1607) were re-hung and increased to five in 1960, with the addition of one recast from a bell of the old Derwent Chapelry removed when the Ladybower reservoir was made.

A unique feature at Chelmorton is the telephone kiosk standing on the last remnant of the village green. It is stone-built and slated, and the only one of its kind in existence.

Above the village rises the flat-topped **Chelmorton Low** (1,458 feet), whence there is an extensive view of the whole Wye Valley. On the summit are prehistoric barrows. Eastward, on the summit of Five Wells Hill, is a tumulus, with Neolithic cist, which has been scheduled for protection as an ancient monument. A path crosses the hill to Taddington, on the Buxton–Bakewell road (buses).

Two miles south-east of Chelmorton is **Flagg,** an interesting Derbyshire village which is, on the Tuesday following Easter, the scene of the High Peak Hunt point to point races. Buxton can be regained thence by the bus passing along the Bakewell road, reached by a by-road from the village.

OTHER EXCURSIONS FROM BUXTON

I.—TO LUDCHURCH AND THE ROACHES

These are situated some 8-9 miles south-west of Buxton. The Buxton–Leek buses will carry outward-bound pedestrians to Flash Bar and take them back from Upper Hulme, south-eastward of the Roaches.

The first part of the route is by the Leek road along the flank of **Axe Edge** (p. 34), passing the head of the Dove.

Less than half a mile beyond Dove Head Farm is **Flash Bar,** where stands the *Traveller's Rest* (1,535 feet above sea-level). A little beyond the Inn we take the right-hand turning for Quarnford, otherwise—

Flash

a small but well-kept hamlet which has changed little over the past century. Tucked within the shelter of Oliver Hill to the north it is nevertheless 1,500 feet above sea level thus allowing its Parish Church the distinction of occupying the highest site of any church in England. It is set in some of the wildest countryside of the Peak District. The villagers are proud of their village hall which they erected themselves with assistance from student volunteers. The only water supply is from a spring at the roadside. In the garden of one cottage are metereological instruments and readings are telephoned every two hours by the owner to Manchester airport.

Some years ago the village was famous as a place of forbidden sporting events such as prize fighting and cock fights. The close Cheshire and Derbyshire border offered a quick retreat should authority venture to intervene; the remains of two cock-fighting pits are still to be seen. At one time the cottage industry was " buttoning," the covering of wooden buttons with cloth, while it is said that counterfeit or " Flash " coins of pewter were once made here. An interesting cattle market is held on the last Friday of the month throughout the summer.

Millers Dale (*J. Salmon*)

Tideswell (*F Frith*)

The Winnats Pass (*F. Frith*)

At Bakewell (*F Frith*)

From Flash two roads run to the south-west. The shorter (that to the right) goes straight down a lane. It is useful for pedestrians, but is too rough for vehicles, which follow a more circuitous route through a pretty valley, in company with one of the earliest tributaries of the Dane. The roads re-unite and, a little beyond the junction, descend to the *Manor Farm*, about 2 miles from Flash Bar by the shorter route.

For Ludchurch follow the lane between Manor Farm and the river as far as the iron gate leading to *Gradbach Mill*. *Cars should not be taken more than a few yards inside the gate, except in dry weather. In wet weather the surface of the lane to the mill becomes dangerously slippery.* Pass between the derelict mill and the mill-house, climb a few rough stone steps in front, and take a well-beaten footpath for nearly half a mile through several stiles, keeping the stream on the right all the time, and the wood on the hillside, at the top of which is Ludchurch, in front. On nearing the wood, cross a footbridge over a tributary stream coming down the hill from the left. In a few yards you are in the wood and are confronted by three paths. Take the middle one, which in a few yards more leads on to a cart track running through the wood from left to right. Follow this to the right, thus making an easy ascent to the top of the wood, where on the right is an isolated mass of rocks called, from their resemblance to a ruined stronghold, the *Castle Cliffs*. At this point turn sharply to the left along a narrow footpath, and in a few hundred yards the entrance to *Ludchurch*, which is a cleft in the side of the rock, is reached. The walk from the Manor Farm to Ludchurch takes about half an hour.

Ludchurch

(properly *Lud's Church*) is said to be named after one of the earliest preachers of the Reformation. It is a rocky rift in the side of the hill, a quarter of a mile long and ranging from 30 to 50 feet in depth. Placed near the western extremity of an extensive moorland district, anciently known as the Back Forest, Ludchurch long afforded means of shelter and concealment to outlaws and disaffected people, criminals and rebels. Tradition says that here services were conducted by Friar Tuck in the presence of Robin Hood and his merry men; also that the Young Pretender, retreating in the '45, slept a night in it; and it is certain that some of the Lollards met here for worship during the persecutions in the reign of Henry V.

The entrance is overshadowed by rocks and mountain-ash and other trees. The path first leads to an almost circular compartment, surrounded by rocky masses of considerable height. Some time-worn steps then lead down to a long and narrow chasm with lofty sides. The ravine terminates in a deep hole, whence descends the *Cavern of Ludchurch*, about which little is definitely known.

So near are the opposite cliffs in parts of Ludchurch, and so completely is the chasm hidden by foliage, that horsemen have ridden close to its edge before becoming aware of danger. It is on record that Squire Trafford, of Swythamley, when out with the hounds, once found himself so unexpectedly near the brink of Ludchurch that to save his life he, by voice and spurs, forced his horse to jump the cleft. The feat was safely accomplished and the spot still bears the name of *Trafford's Leap*.

Leaving the chasm, we come in sight of—

The Roaches

(or Roches), a fantastic ridge of rocks south-eastward of Ludchurch, crowning the wild tract of moorland in which that chasm is situated. The ridge is three miles long and about a mile wide. It overlooks the valley of the Dane, in which woods and moors and pastoral scenery are happily blended. Framing the picture are the town of Leek, Rudyard Lake, Swythamley Hall, Mow Cop, and Congleton Edge. The rocks are of millstone grit; and the country folk declare that they stand on the spot where they were left by the Flood.

The Roaches are private ground, but there is a good walk along the lane on their western side for about 4 miles to Upper Hulme, on the main Buxton-Leek road (*buses*). This lane gives good views of the rocky ridge and of the countryside out to Leek and beyond.

Between the Roaches and Leek is the small Tittesworth reservoir created by the Potteries Water Board by enlarging the New Pool. In time to come when surrounding greenery has grown, it will appear a most attractive sheet of water.

II.—TO LEEK AND RUDYARD LAKE

These are in the same direction from Buxton as are Ludchurch and the Roaches. Leek is about 13 miles from Buxton, from which buses ply.

Leek

Banks.—*District, Martins* and *Midland*, all in Derby Street; *Westminster*, St. Edward Street and Derby Street; *Barclays*, Haywood Street.

Early Closing Day.—Thursday.
Hotels.—*See* Introduction, p. 10.
Population.—19,310.
Post Office.—St. Edward Street.

Leek is an old and important town in Staffordshire, standing on a declivity above the Churnet; a considerable area of Leek Rural District is included in the Peak National Park.

Through Protestant refugees settling in the town, Leek became one of the seats of the silk manufacture. One of the attractions is the Market, held on Wednesdays, under a charter granted by King John in 1208 to the Earl of Chester, who was at that time the Lord of the Manor. It is still a function quite in the manner of the olden days, being attended by farmers and their wives from places miles around, as well as by keen traders from the Potteries. The Market Hall is a covered market in which shops have recently been constructed: at the other end of the town, off Junction Road, a cattle market is held on Wednesdays.

The **Parish Church** (dedicated to Edward the Confessor) is believed to date from the end of the thirteenth century. Noteworthy features are the fine pinnacled tower and the stalls and stained glass. From the churchyard may be obtained a fine view of the Roaches and of Cloud End, near Congleton, and from this point, for a few days at Midsummer, a *Double Sunset* may be observed. The sun first disappears behind Cloud End and shortly afterwards reappears on the north side for a few minutes, before it sinks below the horizon.

Leek, however, is mainly of interest to tourists by reason of its proximity (about 3 miles north-west) to—

Rudyard Lake

The lake, over 2 miles long and most picturesquely situated, was constructed in 1793, to serve as a reservoir for the Trent and Mersey Canal, by building across the valley a huge dam to hold back the overflow waters of the river Dane and its feeders. The lake is well stocked with fish, and anglers' tickets are issued at the *Hotel Rudyard*. The Hotel offers good food and accommodation. Boats and motor-launches can be hired and the lake shore is a favourite picnic ground. Some good sailing can be had. Cliffe Park Hall, on the west side of the lake, is a popular Youth Hostel.

The picturesque village which gives the lake its name was also the name-place of Rudyard Kipling. His father, when a young man, was employed as an artist in the china works at Burslem. In the happy days of his courtship many visits were made to Rudyard Lake, and it was in consequence of the parents' pleasant memories of those outings that the son, who was to win such reputation by his pen, received his Christian name.

III.—TO MACCLESFIELD

Banks.—*Barclays*, Market Place; *District*, Jordangate; *Martins*, Park Green; *Midland*, Mill Street; *Westminster*, Chestergate; *Williams Deacon's*, Chestergate; *National Provincial*, Market Place; *Stockport & Dist. Trustee Savings*, Market Place.

Early Closing Day.—Wednesday.
Hotels.—*See* Introduction, p. 10.
Market Days.—Tuesday, Friday and Saturday.
Population.—37,610.
Post Office.—Castle Street.

Macclesfield is a very ancient town, 12 miles west of Buxton. Jordangate, Chestergate and Churchwallgate (now named Church Street) perpetuate the names of the principal gates in the walls which formerly surrounded the town, but which were destroyed in Cromwellian times.

Macclesfield is famous as the seat of the silk trade, which was introduced on a large scale about 1790. As the town developed and transport improved, it became the acknowledged centre of the silk industry. Today, however, there are many other established industries.

The most prominent building is **St. Michael's Church,** founded in 1278 by Queen Eleanor. In 1740 the spire was removed and the present square tower erected. The south aisle, built by Thomas Savage, Archbishop of York, is known as the Savage Chapel, and contains several effigies of that family. In the Chapel of the Leghs of Lyme are ancient monumental tablets. The most interesting is that in memory of Perkin à Legh, beheaded by Henry IV.

Narrow streets flank the church—one of them mounting by 108 steps. From the Market Place, King Edward Street leads to one of the oldest buildings in Macclesfield—the Unitarian Chapel, built in 1689.

The **West Park,** situated on the outskirts of the town and approached by way of Chestergate and Prestbury Road, has at its entrance a **Museum** containing valuable paintings, exhibits connected with the silk industry, and many objects of general interest. In this park are such noteworthy objects as the old Market Cross and Stocks, monoliths from Ridge Hill and an enormous boulder supposed to have been carried by an iceberg from the coast of Cumberland to the vicinity of its present position. Barnaby Week, which is the annual local holiday (originally the week including St. Barnabas' Day), is now the week containing June 24, except when that date falls on a Saturday, in which case it is the week following.

One of the most picturesque and romantic villages in the neighbourhood is **Gawsworth,** situated four miles south-west of Macclesfield by the Congleton Road.

Gawsworth is famous for its medieval church, a beautiful building in an incomparable setting. The chancel possesses splendid memorials to the Fitton family including the kneeling effigy of Mary Fitton, the supposed " Dark Lady " of Shakespeare's Sonnets. A particularly picturesque feature of the village is the old Fish-Ponds known as the " Silent Pools ". In a wood near by is the grave of an eccentric Gawsworthian, one Samuel Johnson (d. 1773, aged 82), who dubbed himself " Lord Flame ". The villagers however named him " Maggoty Johnson " and the wood in which he lies is still known as " Maggoty Johnson's " wood. (It now belongs to the National Trust.)

Gawsworth Old Hall is a fine half-timbered building dating from the fifteenth and sixteenth centuries. It was the ancient home of the Fitton family and possesses a well preserved tilting ground in the park.

The Old Rectory, coeval in date, has a noble Great Hall over thirty feet high.

IV.—TO DOVEDALE *via* ALSTONFIELD

Proceeding through Higher Buxton, and passing the western end of the Duke's Drive, we enter a reach of road as straight as a dart for a couple of miles. Three miles from Buxton we bear off to the right past Brierlow, with its quarries, and, on the left a mile farther, a road leading to the village of **Earl Sterndale,** which has an inn famed for its sign of *The Quiet Woman,* who is represented by a headless figure.

On the right two remarkably steep heights have appeared like huge natural fortresses. They are known respectively as **Parkhouse Hill** and **Chrome Hill.** Through **Glutton Dale,** "a Highland pass in miniature," we cross the *Dove,* leave Derbyshire and climb towards—

Longnor

a small Staffordshire market town, a mile from the river, and on the main road from Bakewell to Leek. Its churchyard contains a remarkable variety of quaint epitaphs.

Beyond Longnor, continuing southward, we cross the *Manifold* and in 3¾ miles turn left to pass near **Ecton Hill,** on which are mines that in the eighteenth century yielded large quantities of copper. The mines are now abandoned as there remains so little workable copper or lead.

Recrossing the Manifold at Hulme End, about 10 miles from Buxton, the road divides. The branch to the left goes to Hartington, for Beresford Dale (p. 145); that to the right goes on for 3 miles to—

Alstonfield

an attractive parish with prehistoric barrows, a fine church with a pinnacled tower and an Elizabethan Manor House, dated 1587 and now used as a farm house. On the river bank is the three-hundred-year-old Fishing House built by Charles Cotton and inhabited by him with his friend Izaak Walton. There is good angling near Alstonfield. The church of St. Peter was a Saxon foundation and, although the present structure is late Tudor in style, traces remain of earlier periods. Objects of interest are the Charles Cotton pew at the east end of the north aisle; a pew dated 1637 standing near the pulpit; and a monument to Rogerus Farmer, who died in 1682.

From Alstonfield the road bears to the left to drop into the valley of the Dove at **Lode Mill** (p. 140), half a mile above Mill Dale and about midway between Dovedale and Beresford Dale. The village of Alsop-en-le-Dale lies a mile beyond the river. Dovedale is described on pp. 139–144.

V.—TO DOVEDALE *viâ* ALSOP-EN-LE-DALE

The most direct route from Buxton to the northern end of Dovedale is by the Ashbourne road as far as **Alsop-en-le-Dale** (about 15 miles). Alsop village, a model of cleanliness, stands about half a mile to the east of the main road, and some little distance below, but is worth the detour by those with time in hand. It may be reached from the old station by a field path crossing two fields and commands pleasant views of the village. The church possesses some interesting Norman work.

The lane opposite the old station leads to Lode Mill (p. 140); but for Dovedale proper take the field path (indicated by signpost). On the opposite side of the road to which this pathway leads is a gap in a wall, giving entrance to grassy undulating fields, and a well-defined cart-track. Passing by a farm and prominent plantations of trees, the track leads up to the farmyard of *Hanson Grange*. The visitor is now close to the entrance to the Dale, which is gained by the path to the left of the farm by a stile. But for a view of the valley enter the farmyard and take path to the right.

Those who wish to enter the Dale at its southern end follow the Ashbourne road beyond Alsop-en-le-Dale to the gates of **Tissington** (*see* p. 149), opposite which a lane on the right leads in about 1½ miles to the village of Thorpe. Walkers will find an attractive footpath out of the lane (right) about a quarter of a mile from the main road. Dovedale is fully described on pp. 139–144.

VI.—TO TIDESWELL AND EYAM

Both Tideswell and Eyam are on the Buxton–Sheffield bus service and therefore convenient of access.

Motorists and cyclists leave Buxton by the Bakewell road, which is followed for nearly 5 miles; then turn off to the left, passing Blackwell, and descend into Miller's Dale (*see* also p. 45). Turn to the right, down the valley, and fork left at the *Angler's Rest Inn* to climb the hill, passing the entrance to Ravenstor Youth Hostel (National Trust) to Tideswell. A lane diverging to the left just past Miller's Dale Church provides a shorter, but hillier, route for walkers.

Tideswell

is said to derive its name from an ebbing and flowing well. Market rights have existed here since the year 1250.

The grey little town is chiefly visited on account of its ancient **Parish Church,** a fine cruciform building known from its size and beauty as the "Cathedral of the Peak," and well deserving the honour. (Well dressing nearest Sunday to 24th June. Principal Sunday service at 9.30 a.m.)

The Church is dedicated to St. John the Baptist and consists of a nave, with side aisles, north and south transepts and chancel. The lofty Perpendicular tower is surmounted by embattled turrets with curious crocketed spires. The church was erected late in the fourteenth century, at a time when Decorated architecture was giving place to the Perpendicular, and there have been no additions to the main fabric since 1400. The font and the chancel screen and gates are all of that epoch.

The entrance is by the north door. The windows for the most part retain their original stone tracery and the font is of the same age as the church. The old rood screen has been restored to its original design, and in the transepts and at the west end are modern screens which match it. The large niches in the chancel, which have remained empty since the Reformation until 1950, are now decorated with exquisitely carved wood figures.

The north transept contains the old **Guild Chapel** (St. Mary's, now known as the Lady Chapel). In it are ten of the original chancel stalls, discovered and placed there during the restoration of the church. A recent addition, 1952, are the beautiful figures of the "Madonna and Child" in the niche.

The south transept contains two chantry chapels—the **De Bower Chapel** and the **Litton (or Lytton) Chapel,** formerly belonging to the progenitors of the celebrated novelist. In the south aisle, near the Litton Chapel, is a perfect brass of *Robert de Lytton* and his wife (1488). In the De Bower Chapel are the recumbent effigies of *Sir Thurston de Bower* and his wife (about 1395), and also two windows worthy of notice. On the wall, too, just near the twelfth-century bell, is a tablet to *Thomas Statham*, who raised a troop to support Charles I against the "tyrannies of impious regicide." In the centre of the spacious chancel is the restored slab tomb of *Sir Sampson Mevirill* (1462). Note the emaciated effigy below. On the next step is a brass representing *Bishop Pursglove* (1579) in the sacerdotal vestments of pre-Reformation times. Just within the sacrarium is the tomb of *Sir John Foljambe*, who died in 1358. It is marked by a modern brass, the original having been lost nearly two centuries ago. At the eastern end of the chancel is the original stone reredos. The tracery around the sedilia and the piscina is very beautiful.

Above the south porch, and approached by a newel staircase, is a parvise, or watching chamber. On each side of the porch are two large incised crosses, about five feet from the ground, which may be consecration crosses.

The principal road through Tideswell meets the main road from Manchester and Chapel-en-le-Frith on the one hand to the Derwent Valley and Chesterfield on the other in little more than half a mile, at the *Anchor Inn*. For Eyam turn to the right and $1\frac{1}{2}$ miles farther, at the *Three Stags' Heads*, branch to the left from a road to Monsal Head (p. 80) and Bakewell.

The Eyam road shortly begins to descend the beautiful little **Middleton Dale,** the limestone rocks rising into towers and spires on its northern side in a manner reminiscent of Dovedale, though on a smaller scale. In $2\frac{1}{2}$ miles from the fork a road goes off to the left and ascends through the wood-filled ravine of Eyam Dale to—

Eyam

(pronounced to rhyme with " steam "), a picturesque village which is much visited on account of those who have justly won the title of **" The Brave Men of Eyam."**

At the time when the Great Plague of 1665 was raging, a box of clothes was sent from stricken London to a tailor in Eyam. The person who opened it was attacked by the plague and died. The pestilence rapidly spread through the village and five-sixths of the population of 350 died in the course of thirteen months. But a hero arose in the person of William Mompesson, the rector. The terrified villagers were naturally anxious to flee from the infected area; but the rector, realizing the possibility of the spread of the plague far and wide by the flight from Eyam, resolutely set to work, assisted by his wife and by Thomas Stanley, the previous minister, who had been ejected for nonconformity, but who had remained in the village, to persuade his parishioners to keep within their own village area. So strong were the rector's character and influence that he completely succeeded, and the plague was stayed at the limits of the place. His wife was attacked and died, and her tomb may now be seen close by the Runic Cross. It was his mournful duty to bury within a few months the great majority of his parishioners, but he resolutely kept to his work. By an arrangement with the Earl of Devonshire, food was placed on distant rocks for the use of the villagers, and carried by them each day to Eyam at a stated hour. At last the plague ceased; and the many dead, and a few living, with the devoted rector in forefront, have a place to-day in the records of English heroism.

Mr. Mompesson's chair is shown in Eyam Church in the sanctuary and close by is a large illuminated book on which are inscribed the names of the plague victims. The cottages just to the west of the Church, where the epidemic is supposed to have started, are known as the Plague Cottages. Farther along the road is the seventeenth-century Eyam Hall. From the kitchen door may be obtained the key for access to **Cucklet Delf** (*closed on Sundays, except Plague Sunday: entrance by gate in iron railings immediately opposite Hall*). It is situated in a secluded dell in which may be seen the jutting crag known as the **Pulpit Rock,** from which the Rector preached to the brave people of Eyam when the church was closed from fear of infection. A yearly service and procession from the Church to Cucklet Delf on the last Sunday in August commemorates his memory, and is attended by a great many people. "**Mompesson's Well**" (p. 59) is three-quarters of a mile to the north of the village.

Eyam Church consists of a tower dating from the early part of the seventeenth century, chancel, and nave with north and south aisles. It stands on a Saxon foundation and retains a Saxon Font (in the vestry) in addition to the Norman Font—other Norman traces are the two pillars on the north side. Note the original tie beams and the bosses of the roof and the squint behind the pulpit. Over the south doorway of the chancel is a sun-dial which will deeply interest the meteorologist, however much it may puzzle  ordinary people. The Churchyard is pleasantly embowered in foliage, chiefly that of lime trees. It contains two objects of especial interest—a *Saxon Cross* about eight feet high, embossed, like the one at Bakewell, with circles curiously working into each other and with the figures of the Virgin and Child and angels, and the tomb of Catherine Mompesson, the devoted and ill-fated wife of the clergyman whose heroism we have already recorded. Both these memorials are near the south-east angle of the church—the latter, an altar-tomb. In 1962 an interesting series of wall paintings were discovered beneath successive coats of plaster.

Eyam has a pleasant village green on which are well-preserved stocks. A well-dressing festival is held on the last Saturday of August, and a sheep-roast and carnival on the first Saturday of September.

The road down Middleton Dale continues to **Stoney Middleton,** a charming little village over which, on the north side, the limestone cliffs fairly frown. The south side hereabouts is unfortunately much spoiled by quarrying. The road goes on to Calver in the Derwent valley, the transition from the narrow dale to the open valley being quite sudden.

Eyam lies on the southern slopes of the hills confining the western side of the Derwent valley as it flows down from Hathersage. North of the village the hill-tops comprise a fine heathery moorland, with splendid views across to the Pennine Edges, and many visitors find it difficult to resist the urge to explore this piece of country.

Eyam to Hathersage by Eyam Moor (4 miles).—Take the foot-path through the churchyard and at its end turn to the right along the road which, starting from the village street about 400 yards west of the church, curves rapidly upward and climbs to the top of the moor. A hundred yards beyond the first road on the left and ¾-mile from Eyam we pass on the same side **Mompesson's Well,** one of the places appointed for the reception of food during the plague. It is in a grassy *cul-de-sac*, open to the road, and some 40 yards long. Continuing along the rising road we suddenly breast the rise and are greeted by a splendid view across the Derwent valley to the Edges. Then the road runs into **Sir William Road,** a remarkable thoroughfare, which rises in a bee-line for 1¾ miles from a height of 850 feet, above the Derwent Valley, to 1,324 feet. It may have been named after Sir William Peveril (*see* p. 68), or may even have been a road before that vassal of the Conqueror was granted the Peak District. In its highest part it crosses Sir William Hill (1,370 feet): it was once the road from Tideswell and Peak Forest to Sheffield. From opposite the end of the road up from Eyam a track half-left leads across the heather to Stoke Ford and **Abney**; for Hathersage follow the well-marked footpath to the right across Eyam moor. From the moor the rich Derwent valley and the rocky Edges to the right of Hathersage compose a charm-ing landscape. The track descends to a lane which joins the main valley less than a mile south of Hathersage. On the way the little **Highlow Valley** to the left, rich in wood and pasturage, looks its best.

Motorists and cyclists may make a pretty if somewhat rough way down to Hathersage by turning down Sir William Road for about ¾-mile and then taking the shady lane on the left, which is that mentioned above. The going is very poor, however, and those at all nervous about springs should follow Sir William Road to its foot at Grindleford Bridge, there turning to the left.

For **Hathersage,** *see* p. 76.

Eyam to Hathersage by Bretton Clough (5½ miles).—Take the road proceeding west from the village for about a mile, then turn up a narrow lane on the right and follow the footpath above some old mine workings to the *Barrel Inn* at **Bretton,** on Sir William Road (*see* p. 59). At Bretton is one of the simpler type of Youth Hostel. There are wide and rather desolate views across the typical " stone wall " country of these limestone uplands. Turn to the right past the Inn and continue straight forward, ignoring a lane to the right, across some fields to the brink of **Bretton Clough.** The ground falls very steeply to the floor of the glen; a number of isolated hillocks clothed with trees rise in the foreground and a diversified view is spread out on all sides. Follow the zigzag path down to the bottom and continue along the clearly-marked track downstream, passing some ruined farm buildings on the way, to **Stoke Ford.** Here the stream is crossed by a bridge. Turn through the gate and cross the tributary stream, then follow the track obliquely up the hillside. On reaching the highway turn right for Hathersage (about 2 miles). *Highlow Hall*, once a residence of the Eyre family, is passed in about ½-mile on the right. This road joins the busy high road up the Derwent Valley at the *Plough Inn*, where we turn left for Hathersage. The scenery in Bretton Clough, and especially the view of it from above, are as choice as anything of the kind in Derbyshire.

THE HIGH PEAK DISTRICT

Edale—Hope—Castleton—Hathersage

This, considered by many to be the finest part of the Peak District, lies to the north-east of Buxton. It is readily accessible from Manchester and Sheffield by bus, but buses from Buxton do not approach nearer than Chapel-en-le-Frith, except by making a long detour.

BUXTON TO CASTLETON BY ROAD

Buxton is left by way of Fairfield, $2\frac{1}{2}$ miles beyond which is the quarrying village of—

Dove Holes
so called on account of the large number of small water-swallows in the neighbourhood. In local dialect it is " Darf holes "—*i.e.*, " dwarf holes."

A Water-Swallow is a hole in which a stream disappears, descending into an underground channel and emerging to the surface at a distance, in some cases, of several miles. In many instances, when the streams are full, the swallow is unable to receive the whole of the water, and the diminished flow continues its course along the surface; but in dry weather the entire stream disappears.

Lying on the right of the main road is the ancient circle known as the " Bull Ring," scheduled for protection as an ancient monument, though to-day no stones remain to show its link with the past.

The road turns sharply to the right from that to Chapel at the foot of the hill opposite a former inn and half a mile farther reaches the **Ebbing and Flowing Well,** a " Wonder of the Peak." This is by the roadside, on the right hand, almost opposite the gates of Bennetston Hall.

After much rain the phenomenon, although not as marked as it used to be, takes place every ten or fifteen minutes, the water issuing from a small aperture in the side of the hillock on which the well is located. The ebb and flow is believed to be due to a curved conduit through which the water has to pass. One limb of this conduit becomes gradually filled with water as it drains to the surface. At the same time the water rises to the same level in the other limb of this natural syphon; and when the second limb has become filled to its farther extremity the flow takes place and continues until both limbs of the conduit are emptied, when the flow ceases, and the syphon has to be again filled. The visitor must not, however, expect to see a picturesque fountain or anything romantic. The well looks what it really is—nothing more than an ordinary watering-place for cattle, with on one side a stone wall.

According to Charles Cotton's *Wonders of the Peak*, 1683:

> " . . . whether this a Wonder be; or no
> 'Twill be one, Reader, if thou seest it flow,
> For having been there ten times, for the nonce
> I never yet could see it flow but once! "

At the top of the hill is a hamlet bearing the singular name of **Sparrowpit.** By making a digression to the right here we can visit the rather bleak village of **Peak Forest.** The Church, founded by the Countess of Devonshire, is dedicated to King Charles the Martyr. By virtue of Royal Grant it had a " peculiar " jurisdiction, and thus became a kind of Gretna Green, for the priest could celebrate a valid marriage ceremony between " any persons," from " anywhere," at " any time "! At one period about 100 marriages a year were solemnized here.

This locality was formerly the centre of a huge Royal Deer Forest; now it is practically one vast quarry.

From Sparrowpit the Castleton road lies straight on. After a mile and a half there is a track on the right leading to **Eldon Hole,** another " Wonder of the Peak." It is a chasm on the southern side of **Eldon Hill** (1,543 feet) and was formerly looked upon with awe as being fathomless, so that Sir Aston Cokayne, of Ashbourne, wrote in 1658—

> " Here, on a hill's side steep
> Is Eldon Hole, so depe
> That no man living knows
> How far its hollow goes."

In 1780, however, an explorer discovered the bottom at a depth of 180 feet. The hole is a natural cavern having its roofs and walls covered with stalactite deposits—in some places smooth and white as marble, in others like frosted silver—the rougher portions of the rock assuming all sorts of fantastic shapes. The cavern can only be descended by rope ladders.

In a mile or so the main road reaches its highest point near **Winnats Head** at 1,351 feet. Unless it is desired to visit the Blue John Mine and the Treak Cliff Cavern, those who desire to approach Castleton on foot should here turn off to the right and descend the **Winnats Pass** (p. 74). The road is too steep for cars. From Winnats Head the main road joins a road from Chapel along the side of Rushup Edge and skirts the foot of Mam Tor, passing the **Blue John Mine** (p. 72), and after a hairpin bend passes the **Treak Cliff Cavern** (p. 72). Before reaching Castleton a lane leads sharply back to the **Speedwell Cavern** (p. 71) and the Winnats.

BUXTON TO HOPE BY RAIL

Those who reach Castleton by railway from the west travel *viâ* Chinley over the **Dore and Chinley Line,** "the most tunnelled bit of railway in this or any other country." As already mentioned, over four miles of the twenty which lie between the two places from which it is named are run through the bowels of the earth. In its open part it traverses two beautiful valleys—Edale and the Hope Valley.

One of the tunnels—the *Cowburn*—is entered some 2½ miles from Chinley Junction. It is 3,700 yards in length, and lies 900 feet below the surface of the long hill through which it is driven. A mile or so from the eastern end of the tunnel is the old-world village of—

Edale

At Fieldhead there is an Information Centre of the Peak Planning Board. There is also a headquarters of Warden Service, which patrols moorland areas now open to public access. There is a small camp site with accommodation for about 40 people.

The village gives its name to the charming Vale of Edale (p. 42). Radiating from the station are delightful walks, through scenery unsurpassed in the Peak District. For the walk by Jacob's Ladder and Edale Cross to Hayfield or the *Snake Inn, see* pp. 41–2.

The high ground south of Edale Station and separating Edale from Castleton commands fine views of the Vale of Edale and the Hope Valley, the latter including Castleton and the picturesque ruins of Peveril Castle; and as already stated (p. 44) provides a splendid ridge walk all the way from Rushup Edge to Lose Hill, descending thence to Hope. Or one can descend directly from Hollins Cross to Castleton.

At the lower end of Edale is—

Hope

a very ancient village, near the junction of the *Noe* with the *Styx*, sometimes called the *Peak's Hole Water*, because it flows out of Peak Cavern (p. 70). Its principal feature is the **Parish Church** (St. Peter's), built about the fifteenth century, in the Perpendicular style. This fine old church, standing close to

the Noe among sycamore and lime trees, has a squat tower surmounted by a broad spire. The entrance has a parvise over the porch, with a canopied niche containing a figure of St. Peter. The transepts and chancel are surmounted by an embattled parapet, with crocketed pinnacles. There are some quaint gargoyles, while the shaft of a Saxon cross stands near the south porch. In the interior of the church are to be seen a Norman font and a well-preserved carved oak pulpit dating from 1652. The *Old Hall Hotel* opposite was formerly the seat of the Balguys, a family possessing extensive estates in the neighbourhood in the seventeenth century.

Surrounded as it is by **Mam Tor,** or the Shivering Mountain (1,700 feet, *see* p. 74) and the curiously-named **Lose Hill** (1,563 feet) and **Win Hill** (1,523 feet), there is no vale in the Peak District more beautiful than that of Hope, though others may be grander and more rugged. On the slopes of Lose Hill is *Moor Gate*, a guest-house of the Co-operative Holidays Association.

One of the most popular walks from Hope is north-eastward over Win Hill to the Derwent Valley. Take the Edale road, beside the *Old Hall Hotel*. In a quarter of a mile, at a bend in the road, a lane goes down to the river and crosses it just below a weir. Some 200 yards beyond the bridge, stone steps ascend the bank on the right to a path crossing the railway. This path leads up to Twitchill Farm, then bears up to the right, crossing the ridge well to the left of the rocky tor which forms the highest point.

A path, which may be used on sufferance only, leads to **Win Hill Peak,** as the summit tor is called. There is a remarkably wide-spreading view, including the vast Kinder Scout plateau, the wilds of Bleaklow (to the north of it), Derwent Edge and Stanage Edge (across the Derwent Valley), and glimpses of the new Ladybower Reservoir and the rich Woodlands Valley below.

A path, signposted " Yorkshire Bridge," descends through the heather on the north side of Win Hill. Entering a young forest, continue down towards the junction of the two arms of the **Lady-bower Reservoir,** completed in 1945. The branch to the left threads the beautiful Woodlands Valley: a stark new bridge carries the Manchester-Sheffield road over the Derwent Dale arm. Meeting a track from Ashop Farm go to the right. When the track forks, keep to the left and descend, to join the cart-road round the southern side of the reservoir just before reaching the great new dam.

Branch to the left now and go down to **Yorkshire Bridge,** which spans the Derwent, and ascend thence to a road which goes right to Bamford (p. 77). The round from Hope village to Bamford Station is a good 5 miles.

For visitors who come by rail *Hope* is the station which gives access to the villages of Castleton and Bradwell (p. 75).

Castleton

Buses to or from Hope Station, 2 miles; and from Bakewell and Sheffield. **Hotels.**—*See* Introduction, p. 10.

Castleton is not only set amidst picturesque scenery itself, but is a convenient centre for the most mountainous part of the Peak District, whilst its remarkable caverns attract many visitors.

Among the old customs which still linger here is the holding of a carnival on May 29, called *Garland Day*, when there is a procession, with a mounted king and queen, the former carrying a huge garland of flowers, and the village children dressed all in white. A band of music and morris-dancers enliven the nooks and corners of the village, and a Maypole on the market-place becomes the centre of a joyous crowd.

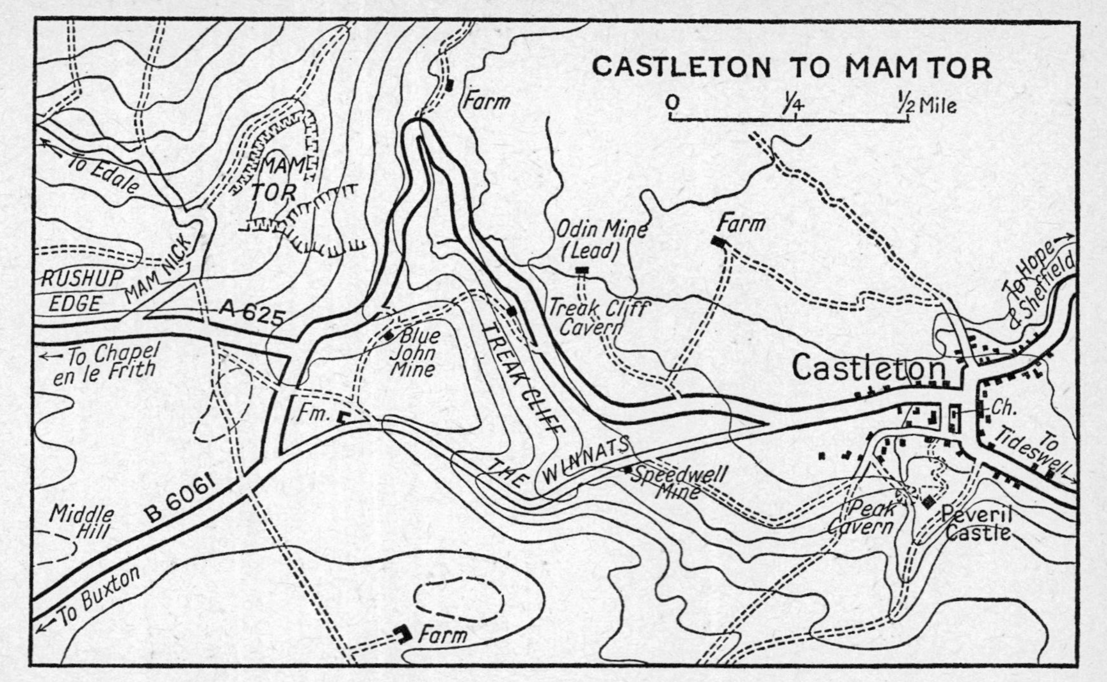

CASTLETON TO MAM TOR
0   ¼   ½ Mile
Farm
To Edale
MAM TOR
Odin Mine (Lead)
Farm
To Hope & Sheffield
RUSHUP EDGE
MAM NICK
A 625
Treak Cliff Cavern
Blue John Mine
TREAK CLIFF
Castleton
To Chapel en le Frith
Fm.
Ch.
To Tideswell
THE WINNATS
Speedwell Mine
B 6061
Middle Hill
To Buxton
Peak Cavern
Peveril Castle
Farm

Sprigs of oak are worn by the villagers, many of whom ascribe the gaiety as commemorating the Restoration of King Charles II, who landed at Dover on May 29, 1660. At sunset the great garland is hoisted by means of a rope to the summit of the church tower, being there secured on the central pinnacle, which it decorates until it is withered.

The **Parish Church** is dedicated to St. Edmund, and dates from the Norman Conquest, when it was built by Peveril, the founder —or restorer, as the case may be—of the Castle. The Church exhibits all the styles of architecture which have prevailed since that period. It consists of chancel, nave with aisles and south porch, and has a fifteenth-century pinnacled tower at the west end. It contains an ancient stone font, and there is a fine Norman archway between nave and chancel. The doors of the old oak pews still bear the names of the occupants in the seventeenth and eighteenth centuries. The vestry contains a good library, the gift of a former vicar, including some valuable and curious works— among others, a copy of the " Breeches " Bible (so called from the unusual rendering of Genesis iii, 7) and a Cranmer Bible.

Castleton obtained its name from its close connection with—

Peveril Castle

(**Admission** charge. **Open** May to September, 9.30 to 7, Sundays from 2 **p.m.**; March, April and October, 9.30 to 5.30, Sundays 2 to 5.30; November to February, 9.30 to 4, Sundays 2 to 4.

The Castle is a fortress which towers above the small grey houses of the village and is a conspicuous feature in any characteristic view of Castleton. The ruin is reached by a zigzag path, starting by a cottage near the south-west corner of the Square. The stronghold is inaccessible on every side save one, and even there the approach is an artificial one, to obviate the severity of the ascent; and the very narrow isthmus connecting the promontory on which it stands with the main ridge of the moorland was guarded by a keep. "The fortress hangs over the mouth of the Devil's Cavern; its founder chose his nest,"

says Sir Walter Scott, "upon the principles upon which an eagle selects her eyry, and built it in such a fashion, as if he had intended it, as an Irishman said of the Martello towers, for the sole purpose of puzzling posterity." Its position was wellnigh impregnable before the discovery of gunpowder.

The lordship was granted, with a number of others in Derbyshire, by William the Conqueror to William Peveril in 1068. The north curtain wall may be ascribed to him and to his son, William, who was dis-inherited in 1155, his estates being forfeited to the Crown. In 1157 Henry II received the homage of Malcolm, King of Scotland, within its walls. He visited it on several occasions, and erected the existing keep at a cost of £135. During the rebellion of the barons against King John, the Castle was garrisoned by the rebels. In the reign of Edward III it passed to the Duchy of Lancaster, of which it still forms a part.

The few remains are very interesting, and the Ministry of Public Building and Works has carried out repairs. The north curtain wall is well preserved and there are parts of the west curtain, which is of a later date. The keep, dating from about 1175, forms a prominent object in the landscape from every direction. St. John Hope describes it as "a characteristic Late Norman rectangular keep, about 60 feet high, and measuring 21 feet 3½ inches by 19 feet 2 inches internally, with walls 8 feet thick." The castle-yard occupied nearly the whole of the summit, and was cut off from the remainder of the ridge by a dry ditch. The gateway, of which some fragments remain, was on the narrow east side. (Portions of the ashlar masonry of the keep are embodied in Castleton Church.)

On the south side of the precipice on which the Castle stands is—

Cave Dale

a beautiful and secluded valley reached by the road which starts from the south-east corner of the village Square and a narrow gap on the right through the limestone wall. The narrow floor is formed mostly of short soft turf. It is a spot which the visitor with time at his disposal should not miss. In the course of an ascent of the Dale delightful views varying with each upward step are obtained of the Castle and the Hope Valley. The Dale emerges on to the moor, where there is a junction of four tracks: Hope and Bradwell—Buxton—Chapel —Castleton. The last may be regained by way of the Winnats (p. 74), with Mam Tor in front of us, increasing in grandeur as we approach the head of the pass, and the fine mass of Rushup Edge keeping guard on our left.

The Caverns

The Caverns, etc.—It should be noted that inspection of the various caves involves certain expenses in guides' fees and that if only one or two visitors share these the cost of visiting one place may be as much as 5s. per head. During the season there is usually no difficulty, as parties are made up every half-hour or so, or even more frequently; but out of the season it is advisable, if economy is an object, to visit Castleton on a Saturday. Parties of school-children, in charge of a master or some responsible person, are admitted at much cheaper rates.

Those who are not perfectly sound in wind and limb should also bear in mind that although the inspection of the Peak Cavern involves practically no steps (the path being more or less level throughout) and the flight of about 100 steps down to the Speedwell Mine is perfectly safe and well lit, the tour of the Blue John Mine involves a descent of some 160 steps and a number of steep passages—and their consequent re-ascent—and the exploration of Treak Cliff Cavern also involves a climb of some 150 feet.

The Caverns usually shown at and near Castleton are four in number, and differ much in character, but the hills have many smaller caves and also old mine shafts. Of their kind these caves are the most remarkable in the country: if they lack the marvellous beauty of the Cheddar Caves, they are also less artificial and commercialized. The Peak Cavern is almost wholly a natural formation, the sole work of man being the enlargement of some of the passages. The Speedwell Cavern, which comes next in point of distance, is rightly regarded as the most sensational. The Blue John Cavern has the finest encrustations, though the more recently opened Treak Cliff Cavern is hardly less remarkable in this respect.

Nearest to the centre of the village is the Peak Cavern. This is reached by a lane commencing alongside the Castleton Youth Hostel at the south-west corner of the Square and passing (right) the **Douglas Museum,** open daily including Sunday (*admission 9d.,* children *4d.*), which is of far greater interest than many more pretentious establishments. There are a number of interesting locks, ancient and modern; beautiful specimens of local minerals and, perhaps most fascinating of all, a collection of miniature models of machinery, buildings, etc.

A few yards beyond the Museum the lane reaches the river known as the *Styx,* or sometimes, from its adventurous upper course, as the *Peak's Hole Water* (of which more is seen when we visit the Peak Cavern). Do not cross the bridge, but turn up the passage between the cottages on the left. A charge of 1d. per person is made for the access through the private garden to the **Russett Well,** a small, crystal-clear pool that is of much greater interest than it superficially appears to be. It is actually part of a mysterious river which has its source up near Buxton, quickly disappears underground, is seen again in the Speedwell Cavern (*see* p. 71), where it drops into the "Bottomless Pit" and is not again seen until it reaches this point. What happens to the waters after plunging into the Bottomless Pit is not known, but by colouring the water in the Pit and noting the time at which the coloured water reaches the Russett Well it has been found that the journey occupies many hours—a very clear indication that the course is extremely tortuous. Below the well, the waters join with those proceeding out of the Great Cavern—another of the underground rivers for which this district is famous.

Returning to the road, cross the bridge and immediately turn left into the riverside path, which leads up between cottages to the entrance to—

The Peak Cavern

(**Open** daily from 10 a.m. to 7 p.m., Sundays to 8 p.m. Evening tours by arrangement (Tel. HOPE 285). **Admission,** Adults 1*s.* 6*d.,* children under 14 years 1*s.* (for minimum party of ten persons).)

The approach is extremely impressive. The sheer limestone cliffs here make a slight recess, above which Peveril's Castle keeps guard. Below the path a slight stream issues from a " swallow "—the same stream which is seen inside the Cavern—then, as the path bears to the right, the huge, semicircular opening of the Cavern confronts us.

This great curiosity, originally known as " the Devil's Hole of Peak," and called the " Devil's Cavern " by Sir Walter Scott, is 200 yards below the surface of the mountain in which natural forces have excavated it.

The cave is entered by a natural arch, 60 feet high, 102 feet wide, and 334 feet in depth. Beyond this hall, which has been utilized as a rope-walk for over 400 years, a narrow low passage, equipped with electric light, conducts the visitor to a spacious opening, called the **Bell-House** or Belfry from a number of round holes in the roof. It is separated from the interior by a stream of water, the *Styx,* which is now passed by a path leading through a passage, but which was formerly traversed in a flat-bottomed punt. The passage leads to the **Great Cave** or **Devil's Cavern,** a spacious chamber, parts of which are estimated to be 200 feet long, 150 feet in width and 100 feet high, the whole being enarched with a magnificence of general effect and a beauty and variety of detail which baffle description. A passage has been discovered leading from this chamber, through the roof, and coming out near to Peveril Castle. The extremity of this hall narrows into a second passage, near the farther end of which is a group of broken rocks which have received the name of **Roger Rain's House,** from the constant trickling of water down their sides. Above Roger Rain's House is the **Orchestral Chamber,** or Chancel, a naturally-formed opening high in the rock, with stalactitic encrustations, and where, on special occasions choral concerts are held. Beyond is **Pluto's Dining Room** and the **Devil's Staircase,** giving access to the perfect natural cloisters known as the **Five Arches** through which the *underground river* flows. Near its source is the Victoria Cavern with a roof so high that it is invisible. Here the practicable exploration of the cavern is brought to a halt. The cavern is now owned by the Duchy of Lancaster.

Leaving the Cavern, follow the path back alongside the stream, cross the bridge and in a few yards turn left along a path which leads to the main road. Here turn left again and keep left at the fork in about a quarter of a mile for—

The Speedwell Cavern

(**Open** daily throughout the year from 10 a.m. to 7 p.m. **Admission,** adults 2*s.*, children 1*s.* Coach and Car Park at the entrance. Refreshments available. Tel. HOPE 512.)

This mine is at the foot of Long Cliff, near the entrance to the Winnats, three-quarters of a mile from Castleton.

Entrance to the cave is gained by an arched vault, closed by a door, whence a descent of 72 feet, made by means of steps floodlit with electricity, leads to a " level," now converted into a subterranean canal, traversed by a large flat-bottomed boat, holding 18 or 20 persons. The canal is a cutting in the rock made towards the end of the eighteenth century by a party of adventurers engaged in mining for lead. After eleven years' effort and the expenditure of £14,000, work was abandoned. The stream which flows through the mine has its source at Perry Foot Well, on the uplands between Castleton and Buxton. After its subterranean journey, it reappears at the Russett Well, little more than half a mile away, in a direct line, but the passage occupies twenty-two hours. The natural outlets of the water are blocked to an extent sufficient to maintain a depth of 3 feet 6 inches. As the boat passes along, the conductor places candles at intervals on the sides of the tunnel, which is so straight that the whole of the lights can be seen from end to end. The effect is very striking.

The narrow passage continues for about 750 yards; then suddenly becomes an enormous gulf, at an immense cavern which was struck during the excavations. The most probable theory is that the cavern was formed by the dissolution of a vein of soft limestone by the water which permeated it. A broad platform, protected by a stout iron railing, has been thrown across the chasm to allow visitors to survey the abyss—"The Bottomless Pit "—in safety and comfort. The noise of the cascading water and the effect of the reflected lights in this cave are most interesting.

Opposite the entrance to the Speedwell Cavern, a footpath provides a short cut to the main road, above which, a few hundred yards to the left, is the entrance to the—

Treak Cliff Cavern

(**Open** all the year daily from 10 a.m. till dusk. Evening tours by arrangement. **Admission,** adults 2*s.*, children 1*s.* Free car park.)

This cavern, first opened to the public in 1935, rivals those of Cheddar in the profuse display of scores of stalactites and the attendant stalagmitic formations. The colour contrasts are indeed astonishing for their delicacy and variety. The most remarkable characteristic of the hill in which it is situated, known as **Treak Cliff,** is that it is the only place in the world where Blue John stone is found. It stands alone at the western extremity of Hope Valley, at the base of Mam Tor, and is isolated by faults and deep ravines on every side. It was while mining for Blue John stone in 1926 that the workers discovered the Treak Cliff Caverns. Visitors are conducted through the old workings, with veins of Blue John stone (*see* p. 14) *in situ*, beyond which are the natural caverns, containing a most remarkable show of stalactites and stalagmites. Curious cave and stalagmite formations have been given the names of *Aladdin's Cave*; *The Dream Cave*; the *Dome of St. Paul's*; the *Witches Cave* and the *Frozen Waterfall*. The cavern is lit by electricity.

About a mile from Castleton, there appears on the left of the road a deep cleft in the cliff: the remains of the **Odin Mine,** one of the oldest and most valuable sources of lead in the district. The Saxons are said to have worked it by aid of convicts, and it was the Saxons who gave the mine its name. The mine is of further interest as marking the junction of the Limestone (to the east) with the Yoredale Shales which are so pronounced a feature of neighbouring Mam Tor. Near the entrance to the mine are some small caves: they are wet, not particularly interesting, and hardly worth the slight toil of reaching them.

The Blue John Caverns

(**Open** daily from 10 a.m. to 6 p.m., Sundays included. **Admission,** adults 1*s.* 6*d.* Children under 14 years 9*d.*; 14-16 years 1*s.* Special rates for parties.)

The Blue John caverns are reached by following the main road as it curves round steeply before the face of Mam Tor. The entrance to the mine will be seen on the left soon after the steepest part of the ascent has been passed. A quick and picturesque route from Castleton is to take the footpath from the top of the Winnats Pass. From Edale a footpath leads through Mam Nick to the Cavern.

The full inspection of the mine entails a descent and corresponding ascent of some 160 steps, as well as of a number of steep gradients. For those to whom such work offers no terrors the visit is well worth while.

The mine takes its name from the very beautiful variety of fluorspar known as **Blue John,** or " The Peakland Jewel," which is found in it. Fluor-spar is generally white. So rare is this bluish-purple mineral that orders for it are always on hand. Tazzas and other works of art made from Blue John grace many palaces and famous houses; a particularly fine example is in the Vatican Library; there is a large one at Chatsworth House, whilst two Blue John vases have been discovered at Pompeii.

" The name was given in contradistinction to a metal-blend known to the old miners as Black Jack. The first stone mined was blue in colour, so Blue John and Black Jack are namesakes. The stone is ' calcium fluoride,' or ' fluor-spar.' Every form is found in Castleton: blue, red, purple, and dark colours, displayed in banded veins of extraordinary richness and beauty. There are 14 distinct varieties, and all are found at different depths from the summit of the hill. I know a vein that runs up within a yard of the surface, and another 280 feet deep, there being twelve intermediate kinds between the two levels. The level seems to determine both the veinings and the colour. Blue John is found only in very small limestone caverns, averaging 6 feet high, and coats the roof, the sides and the floor. The veins run horizontally in seams averaging 2½ inches thick and between the top and bottom vein sulphate of baryta and clay in equal proportions are always found. The last deposit of the series is clay. This points indubitably to the Blue John being a water deposit."—*The Geology of Castleton*, by John Royse.

The principal attractions of this series of caves, the biggest range of natural caverns in Great Britain and extending for over 2 miles, are the large stalactites, the immense variety of shell-fossils embedded in the limestone on its sides, and the uninterrupted range of caverns and Blue John stone.

One of the openings, known as **Lord Mulgrave's Dining-Room,** is 30 feet wide and 150 feet in height. It owes its name to the fact that Lord Mulgrave, who took a great interest in the exploration of the caves and mine, entertained the workmen in it. Vast portions of the sides of the Crystal Waterfall are covered with sparry encrustations of great variety, reflecting most beautifully the illuminations, and presenting the appearance of a great cascade. The dome of the **Crystallized Cavern** is of exceptional beauty and colour. The **Variegated Cavern** is also visited; here dark patches of manganese dioxide (the colouring matter of Blue John) glitter in great profusion.

A green track leading up to the right from the entrance to

the Blue John Mine goes to *Winnats Head Farm,* just above the head of the rugged gorge known as—

The Winnats

a narrow rift in the limestone hills through which climbs the old road to Buxton from Castleton. "Winnats" is a corruption of Wind Gates, a name the pass obtained from the gusts of wind which constantly sweep through. South-west breezes make themselves felt with special force. The view through the great rocky portals presents a scene of magnificent extent and beauty.

The Winnats is one of the few passes which appear more impressive when walked down than when climbed up. The distance from Winnats Head to the Speedwell Mine is about three-quarters of a mile.

Westward of Castleton and above the head of the Winnats rises—

Mam Tor

a hill of very singular aspect, much of the surface presenting the appearance of having been scooped out. The hollows are due to the action of the atmosphere on the siliceous shale and sandstone of which the hill is composed. Exposure to the atmosphere causes the disintegration of the shale and sandstone, which then trickle down into the valley below. On account of this movement the hill is often called the *Shivering Mountain,* and is one of the " Wonders of the Peak."

The view is similar to that from Rushup Edge (*see* p. 44). In the opinion of one writer: " It may be doubted whether there is anything finer to be seen in England than the view from the summit of Mam Tor. It includes almost everything which goes to form magnificent scenery, except water."

To reach the hill proceed as to the Blue John Mine, and then continue along the Chapel-en-le-Frith road: the right fork. About half a mile from the mine one can cross a field on the right by a path to **Mam Nick,** a slight depression on the west side of the hill, or go on a little farther to a road which leads back to the same point. If approaching by way of the Winnats, take the path continuing westward from Winnats Head Farm. It crosses the Buxton road and meets the Chapel road opposite the path above. From the " Nick," Mam Tor is but a quarter of a mile distant, and the way is perfectly plain. The " Nick " provides a very fine surprise view of Edale and the High Peak.

Castleton may be regained from the summit of Mam Tor by the exceptionally fine ridge walk to Hollins Cross, from which a good track descends direct to the village, or by continuing thence over Back Tor to Lose Hill, from which a well-defined track drops down to Hope.

From Castleton a visit can also be paid to the picturesque village of—

Bradwell

2 miles to the south-east by the Tideswell road and a path continuing at the foot of the hills, or 3 miles by taking the road south from Hope. Buses from Bradwell meet the trains at Hope and there are bus connections with Castleton and Sheffield.

The village nestles in rugged picturesque scenery and has much to interest the historian. It was for some years an important lead-mining centre, and it was some of the lead miners who accidentally discovered, in 1807, the fine set of caves now known as the **Bagshawe Cavern,** a few minutes' walk from the centre of the village. One of the most curious of the Derbyshire caves, it is entered from the hillside by a long flight of steps, cut in the rock; and it comprises a number of fantastic chambers, hung with stalactites and sparkling crystals. The caves are open to visitors on Saturday afternoons and Sundays, and at other times by appointment. Northward from the village, a path on the left of Bradwell Brook leads in a mile or so to **Brough.** This is the site of the Roman Station of *Anavio*, now again covered in after excavations had revealed many relics of the Roman occupation; these can now be seen in the museum at Buxton. The Roman Road from Brough to Buxton runs through Bradwell and the *Grey Ditch*; a defensive earthwork can be traced from Bradwell Edge to Micklow Hill near the Bath Hotel, where are the remains of a Roman Bath and a thermal spring. South of Bradwell, at Camphill, Great Hucklow are the headquarters of the Derbyshire and Lancashire Gliding Club. Most weekends gliders can be seen soaring over the place where in the second century the Romans built their fort. South-east of Bradwell one of the most delightful walks is that over Bradwell Edge and *viâ* Robin Hood's Cross to **Abney.** Southwards from **Bradwell** the road ascends **Bradwell Dale,** at the head of which are the remains of the lovely Elizabethan Manor House of Hazlebadge Hall, built by the Vernons in 1549 and now a farmhouse. The road, with towering rocks on either side, continues to the hamlet of Windmill and goes on thence, crossing the Peak Forest–Stoney Middleton road (p. 57) to Tideswell (p. 56), 4 miles away.

Some 5 miles east of Castleton along the main road is—

Hathersage

It is a quaint, old-world village on the slope of a range of hills which protect it from east winds. Hathersage claims to be the place in which Robin Hood's famous henchman, **Little John,** was born; a house, said to have been his, stood near the church. There is little doubt that a man of his stature was buried here. His grave, on the south side of the church, is marked by two small stones, with a yew at head and foot and enclosed by a low iron fence. On being opened in 1782 it disclosed bones of enormous size. The grave was rifled for the second time in the early years of the nineteenth century, and a thigh-bone measuring 32 inches was taken from it. At the same time there was removed from the church, where they had hung for centuries, an ancient cap and bow said to have belonged to the freebooter. Tradition affirms that the outlaw pointed out the spot where he desired to be buried, and directed that his cap and bow should be hung in the church (they are now to be seen in Cannon Hall, Barnsley); and the ballad adds:—

> " His bow was in the chancel hung;
>   His last good bolt they drave
> Down to the rocks, its measured length
>   Westward fro' the grave.
>
> And root and bud this shaft put forth
>   When spring returned anon ;
> It grew a tree, and threw a shade,
>   Where slept staunch Little John."

The fine old **Parish Church** (St. Michael's), mainly fourteenth-century, stands on a height above the village. This fine building is in the Decorated style of architecture, and consists of a nave, aisles and chancel. It has a handsome clerestory, and a beautiful tower of three stages, surmounted by an octagonal spire. The interior contains the altar-tomb of Robert Eyre, of Highlow, an Agincourt hero, and his wife and fourteen children.

Near the church is a circular earthwork, probably dating from the ninth century, known as Camp Green.

Hathersage is generally held to have been the village Charlotte Brontë had in mind when describing the hamlet of

Morton, whither Jane Eyre wandered after her escape from Mr. Rochester and Thornfield Hall; and the lonely house on the Moors where she found shelter is said to be **North Lees Hall,** an Elizabethan mansion, once the residence of the Eyre family, about a mile north of the church, in the valley of the *Hood.* It is now used as a guest house, but retains its mullioned windows, central circular staircase, and other interesting memorials of the age in which it was built. The ruins of the Chapel built by the Eyres in 1686  for the services of the Roman Catholic Church, to which they belonged, and destroyed by a mob in 1688, are to be seen in a field a little below the house.

Moorseats, half a mile up the hill north-east of the church, is thought to be the house where the Rivers sisters, in *Jane Eyre,* lived.

North-west of Hathersage is **Bamford,** which presents a useful starting-point of some good walks in the Derwent Valley, on the rocky Bamford Edge and Stanage Edge to the east, and over Win Hill (*see* p. 64). On the Sheffield road, about $1\frac{1}{2}$ miles above Hathersage, is **Millstone Edge Nick,** called also the **Surprise,** by reason of the lovely scene which suddenly bursts in sight when the spot is approached from the opposite direction. The prospect extends from Mam Tor to Stanage Edge and embraces the pastoral Hope Valley in front, and the wooded valley of the Derwent stretching southwards. Among the details are the Kinder Scout plateau, Win and Lose Hills, on the right of the Hope Valley the entrance to Bretton Clough, and the beautiful Leam Woods rising from the river.

Beside the road just beyond the Surprise is an uncouth mass of weather-stained rock, on which has been bestowed, with more reason than is often the case, the title of the **Toad's Mouth Rock.** About half a mile north of the rock and visible from the Lower Burbage Bridge is **Carl Wark,** a very wonderful Iron Age fort. In the walls are stones of an estimated weight of sixty tons. At the *Fox House Inn* the road from

Castleton to Sheffield meets that coming up from Calver and Baslow (p. 96), in the Derwent Valley.

Those who ascend to this point and wish to vary the return might well turn down to the south through the Longshaw Estate (National Trust), where the Longshaw Sheep Dog Trials attract large numbers of visitors annually in early September, on to Grindleford Bridge, $2\frac{1}{2}$ miles south of Hathersage by the road through the beautiful Derwent Valley passing the fine Youth Hostel of Leam Hall, and also on the Buxton–Tideswell–Sheffield bus route.

BAKEWELL, HADDON HALL AND CHATSWORTH

By Road (*see* below).—In addition to motor-coach trips, there are regular bus services from Buxton, Matlock and Derby to Bakewell, to Haddon Hall and to Rowsley (for Chatsworth).

By Rail.—Bakewell Station is for Bakewell Town. Rowsley Station is the nearest for Haddon Hall (1½ miles) and for Chatsworth (2½ miles). Both stations are on the main London-Derby-Manchester line.

BUXTON TO BAKEWELL BY ROAD

The road runs first through Ashwood Dale (*see* p. 32) and then climbs out of the valley of the Wye. Six miles from Buxton is the long village of **Taddington,** about 1,100 feet above sea-level and therefore among the highest villages in England. The restored fourteenth-century *Church* contains brasses and tombs of the Blackwall family and, projecting from the north wall of the chancel, a stone lectern to hold the book for the singing of the Gospel at Sunday Eucharist. It is still used. In the churchyard is a tall ancient cross shaft. A mile and a half from the village is *The Five Wells Tumulus,* an ancient burying place, now in the charge of the Ministry of Public Buildings and Works.

From Taddington the road descends between lovely woods of **Taddington Dale** (National Trust) to the southern end of—

Monsal Dale

Before setting out it is advisable to enquire about buses from Monsal Head into Ashford or Longstone.

Monsal Dale is of a more open type than the typical Derbyshire Dale and, perhaps because of its contrast, the appeal of its placid waters flowing between smooth green slopes is well-nigh irresistible. The Dale is about 2 miles in length, curving round the hill known as **Fin Cop** (1,072 feet) to the village of Monsal Dale. It is thus very conveniently placed for a circular tour—from Buxton by road, walk through the Dale and return to Buxton by bus, or *vice versa*—and those for whom the walk is not long enough may well continue through to **Miller's Dale** by the private road from Cressbrook Mill (described in the reverse direction on page 45).

Motorists who do not wish to leave their cars and walk through Monsal Dale should, from Ashford, run up to the point on the Tideswell road known as *Monsal Head* (*hotel*): from this there is a lovely view of the Dale.

The road to the right here goes through Little Longstone to **Great Longstone.** The latter consists mainly of a long street bordering the high road, and a pretty green, where there are well-preserved village stocks and a very old cross.

A steep ascent from Great Longstone leads in about a mile to a commanding ridge known as **Longstone Edge,** dividing the valleys of the Derwent and the Wye.

Ashford-in-the-Water

10 miles from Buxton, stands on the Wye, and carries the appendage to distinguish it from the many other Ashfords in the kingdom. Formerly a quiet village, it is popular with visitors, and in spite of a by-pass, has a considerable amount of through traffic. Well dressing and well blessing ceremonies are held on Trinity Sunday and during the week following. There are beautiful bridges and several fine old mansions in the neighbourhood.

The oldest part of the **Church** is the fourteenth-century tower, apart from the Norman tympanum over the south door, which was replaced in its original position in 1869, having been found built into the south wall. The carving represents a tree with a wild boar and a wolf. The shaft of the font is curiously carved to represent the body of a dragon or evil spirit, of which the main portion is suggested as inside the font, while the head and tail are shown outside. "This is perhaps meant to symbolize the influence of baptism over sin."

Hanging in the north aisle of the church are to be seen four garlands of the type carried at the funerals of maidens: according to Dr. Cox the custom was continued until 1820. A wooden frame covered with flowers was carried on the top of a long pole. It was then placed over the pew the girl had occupied in the church. There are similar garlands in the church of South Wingfield and at Matlock. The oak roof of the church is good.

Bakewell

Angling.—*See* p. 16.

Banks.—*Westminster* and *Williams Deacon's*, both in the Square; *Derby Savings Bank*, Bath Street.

Bowling.—Bakewell Town Bowling Club in Bath Gardens.

Buses.—From the Square to Bradwell, Buxton, Castleton, Derby, Hope, Longstone, Matlock, Rowsley, Tideswell, Youlgreave, Monyash and Winster.

Children's Playground, paddling pool, etc.—Rutland Recreation Ground.

Churches and Chapels.—Hours of Sunday services:

Parish Church of All Saints, South Street: 8, 11 and 6.30.

Roman Catholic, Buxton Road.

Methodist, Matlock Street: 10.45 and 6.30.

Plymouth Brethren, Oddfellows Hall.

Society of Friends, off Matlock Street.

Wesleyan Reform, Fly Hill, Buxton Road.

Cricket, Football and **Tennis.**—In Rutland Recreation Ground.

Early Closing Day.—Thursday.

Golf.—Nine-hole course.

Hotels.—*See* p. 10.

Hunting.—Kennels of High Peak Harriers at Shutts Lane. Hunting days Wednesdays and Saturdays.

Market Day.—Monday.

Population.—3,820.

Bakewell is an attractive market town of some agricultural importance, sheltered by hills on the north, east and west; and overlooking rich meadowland to the south. It is the chief town within the Peak National Park, and is an excellent centre for exploring the surrounding countryside, and for visiting the beautiful grounds and mansions of Chatsworth and Haddon Hall.

The name is of Anglo-Saxon origin, and refers to the warm springs of the town. Old records show various forms of the name, that in the Domesday Book being *Badequella,* meaning Bath-Well. But, unlike Buxton, the town has never been developed as a spa. Of the several wells known to have existed, only two remain, the Bath-well in Bath Street, and Holywell (the Pete Well in the Recreation Ground). Traces of Roman occupation have been found in the town: the Roman altar now at Haddon Hall was unearthed near Bakewell.

Although it is clear from the above that the name Bakewell has no etymological connection with cooking, many visitors will associate the name with a well-known pudding or tart. The first Bakewell pudding was made at the *Rutland Arms Hotel,* Bakewell, about a hundred years ago, and was the result of a mistake made by the cook in the mixing of the ingredients —intended for a tart, but resulting in a pudding.

There are some attractive buildings in the town. In the **Market House** are the heraldic shields of the Manners family. Nearby in the Square, on the site of the former White Horse Inn, is the *Rutland Arms Hotel* where Jane Austen stayed whilst revising her *First Impressions*, later to become *Pride and Prejudice*. **Ivy House,** in Church Street, bears the date 1743, and the **Almshouses** on the other side of the road date from 1709. The beautiful **Bakewell Bridge,** with its five Gothic arches and triangular quoins, is one of the oldest bridges in England.

The crowning attraction of Bakewell is its fine—

Parish Church

This large cruciform structure, standing on a commanding site, dates from the beginning of the twelfth century. It is an interesting mixture of various styles of architecture, for while specimens of the original Norman work may be seen in the two western arches of the nave and in the fine west doorway, the rest of the nave and aisles are in the Early English style, introduced in the thirteenth century. Architecturally the exterior is far more satisfying than the interior.

The chancel was rebuilt in the Decorated style in 1300, and sixty years later the **Vernon Chapel** was added as an aisle to the south transept. In this chapel, completely rebuilt in 1841, are buried the families of the Vernons and the Manners, of Haddon Hall; but of the monuments the one that mainly interests visitors is that portraying Sir John Manners and his Lady (*Dorothy Vernon*), (*see* p. 84).

Among other memorials, this part of the church contains an alabaster effigy representing Sir Thomas Wendesley in plate armour. He was killed in 1403 at the Battle of Shrewsbury. One of the oldest and most beautiful monuments is at the end of the south aisle. It portrays in alabaster the figure of Sir Godfrey Foljambe and his wife.

During restoration many pre-Conquest stones were found built into the masonry. They are now preserved in the south porch. The tower, which had become too weak to support the spire, was taken down and rebuilt, with a new spire, in the middle of the nineteenth century, and at the same time the whole central portion of the church was rebuilt.

The great reredos, erected in 1881, at the time the chancel was restored, is beautifully carved. The lower part is of fine Ashford marble; above this are figures in white marble of the Apostles, and crowning the whole is a representation of the Crucifixion, carved in white lime wood, with the city of Jerusalem shown as a background. The font is early fourteenth-century.

Also to be noticed are the fine **Anglo-Saxon Cross,** in the churchyard; the collection of carved slabs, some of them very ancient, in the south porch; and a few quaint epitaphs.

Two miles south of Bakewell on the main A6 Buxton-Matlock road is—

HADDON HALL

The Hall and gardens are open to the public daily (except Sundays) from Good Friday or 1st April to October. Visitors are admitted from 11 a.m. to 6 p.m. (October, 4 p.m.). *Special openings:* Easter Sunday, Whit Sunday and the first Sunday in August from 2 to 6 p.m. There is an admission charge per person. Free car park. Refreshments, luncheons and teas available.

The approach to Haddon Hall is from the main Buxton-Matlock road, between Bakewell and Rowsley. From the Gatehouse the drive crosses the river by a stone bridge, built 1663 and replacing a former structure, just beyond which an excellent view is obtained of the mansion.

Walking Routes.—It is a pleasant two-mile walk over the fields from Bakewell by the footpath over the Iron Bridge below Bakewell Bridge, through the timber-yard and across the bridge over the mill-race. Another path follows the river to Sheep Bridge and forward to the main road.

Haddon Hall, among the most attractive of the ancient manorial dwellings of England, exquisitely beautiful in its surroundings, picturesque in its architecture, and with a halo of romance in its human interest, is situated on a natural elevation above the banks of the Wye.

The fine baronial hall, so impressive in its architecture and surroundings, has inspired—as it could hardly fail to do—artists, poets and novelists by its beauty and the romance of its associations. David Cox, Cattermole and a host of others have painted it; Allan Cunningham, the poet, is generally held to be responsible for the modern version of the story of Dorothy Vernon; while in novels it is the scene of Mrs. Radcliffe's *Mysteries of Udolpho* and of William Bennett's *The King of the Peak*; and the romantic doings of the popular heroine of Haddon are told in *Dorothy Vernon of Haddon Hall*, by Charles Major, and *Sweet Doll of Haddon Hall*, by J. E. P. Muddock.

" Some portions of Haddon Hall are of undoubted Norman origin, and it is not unlikely that even these were grafted on a Saxon erection; the hall porch, the magnificent kitchen and adjoining offices, the banqueting hall, part of the north-east tower, etc., belong to the next later period, from 1300 to about 1380. In the third period, from 1380 to 1470, were added some portions of the chapel and the remaining buildings on the east side of the upper courtyard. The next period, from 1470 to 1530, comprises the western range of buildings in the lower court and the west end of the north range " (*S. C. Hall*).

The chronicles of Haddon tell of peace and hospitality rather than of stirring events. The Vernons derive their name from their original possessions in Normandy; and one of them, marrying in Norman times the daughter of William de Avenall, the owner of the Haddon estate, became the first of the Vernons, Lords of Haddon. A Sir George Vernon, whose monument is in Bakewell Church, was known as " King of the Peak."

For many centuries the story of the Vernons had no place in the national records; squire after squire strove to excel his predecessor in Old English hospitality, and their most fitting memorials are to be found in the great table of the Banqueting Hall and the utensils still preserved in the spacious kitchen. Consequent upon the marriage, in Tudor times, of Dorothy Vernon with John Manners, son of the Duke of Rutland, the estates passed into the possession of the Rutland family.

Until its re-occupation in 1927 by the ninth Duke, the last of the Manners to use Haddon Hall as a residence was John, second Duke of Rutland, popularly known as " the Old Man of the Hill," who died in 1779. His eldest son, the Marquis of Granby, the celebrated general, died before his father.

The Story of Dorothy Vernon

is now generally agreed to have no foundation in fact. But the tradition still sheds, and always will, a halo of human interest around the baronial pile of Haddon Hall. Dorothy Vernon was the youngest daughter and co-heiress of that Sir George Vernon, " the King of the Peak," whose magnificence was princely and whose hospitality profuse. " Tradition," wrote S. C. Hall, one of the best informed of the Haddon chroniclers, " delights to dwell upon her as the most beautiful of all beautiful women, and certain it is that the influence she cast over Haddon is all-pervading. . . . Dorothy Vernon's Door, with its fine bold stone balustrades, has heard the whisper of countless pairs of lovers and been transferred to number-less canvases.

" It was from this beautiful outlet that the heiress of Haddon stole out one night in the moonlight to meet her lover. The story is that while her eldest sister, the affianced bride of the second son of the Earl of Derby, was fortunate in her recognized and open attachment, and petted and made much of, she, the younger sister, was kept in the background because she had formed an attachment to John Manners, son of the Earl of Rutland, a connection opposed by her family.

" Something of the spirit of a wild bird was noticed in Dorothy. She was closely watched, kept almost a prisoner, when, in her own opinion at least, she should have been made free of the woodland. But love laughs at locksmiths. Her lover, disguised as a woodman, lurked in the woods around Haddon for several weeks, obtaining now and then a stolen glance, a hurried word, a pressure of the hand from the beautiful Dorothy.

" At length, on a festal night, when a throng of guests filled the ballroom, when the instruments played in the minstrels' gallery, the young maid of Haddon stole away unobserved, passed out of the door which now bears her name, and crossed the terrace. Horses were waiting, and Dorothy Vernon rode away with young Manners through the moonlight all night, and was married to him next morning in Leicestershire.

The Hall

The route generally taken by visitors is indicated by arrows and is as follows: Lower Courtyard, Chapel, Old Kitchens, Banqueting Hall, Dining Room, Drawing Room, Ante-room and Earl's Bed-room, Long Gallery or Ballroom, State Bedroom, and exit to gardens by Dorothy Vernon's steps. The following descriptive matter is extracted, by permission, from the Official Guide.

The north-west **Entrance Tower** stands at the top of a steep lime-stone slope and dates back mainly to the early sixteenth century, though parts of it and also the massive oak doors are of an even earlier date (1400). On climbing a few steps the visitors come to the **Lower Courtyard.** It is entirely paved with stone and follows the natural slope of the ground on which it is built. On the east side is the fourteenth-century Banqueting Hall and Porch, while the opposite range of buildings is work of the early sixteenth century. Here were housed the many officials of the household. Many of the rooms in the buildings on the north side of the court-yard were originally occupied by the family and several of them have been put to the same use since the Hall was restored by the ninth Duke of Rutland. The line of buildings on the south is broken by the flight of steps leading to a set of rooms known as the Earl's Apartments, built over the old curtain wall which was originally erected in the reign of King John. In the south-west angle of the courtyard is the beautiful octagonal bell-turret of the Chapel. Notice also the sixteenth-century lead rainwater pipes and heads, decorated with the boar's head and the peacock (emblems of the Vernons Dand the Manners respectively).

The **Chapel,** originally dedicated to St. Nicholas, is entered from the south-west angle of the courtyard. In the porch stands an old font, believed to be early Norman, if not Saxon, work. The south aisle of the Chapel is the oldest part of the building and had its origin in the twelfth century, while the tower, west windows and north aisle were added about 1310. Between 1380 and 1470 the building was again enlarged and the chancel added. The chancel was re-roofed in 1624 and at about the same time the wooden pews in the chancel and the altar rail were installed. The Chapel was last restored and refitted by the ninth Duke of Rutland, when, under the direction of Professor E. W. Tristram, many more wall paintings were discovered (some had been partly uncovered in the nineteenth century) and the colours were brought out and intensified.

The wall paintings date from the late fifteenth century. Only a brief mention of the subjects is possible here. On the north wall of the chancel are four paintings representing St. Nicholas; on the south side are several small groups of figures which apparently portray the Holy Family. High up on the south wall of the nave is a large figure of St. Christopher and much of the north wall of the nave and the whole of the west end of the Chapel is covered with a conventional design.

The stone altar in the chancel is the original altar of the Chapel and was repaired in 1930. It shows the Manners' arms impaling Vernon. The nine panels of the Reredos, representing scenes from the Passion, are of alabaster and are work of the fifteenth century. The carved oak cresting along the top is believed to have formed part of the rood-screen, pulled down probably during the seventeenth century. Much of the valuable painted glass in the Chapel was stolen in 1828: enough, however, remains to show how beautiful the windows must have been in their original state. The old stone altar in the south aisle has five consecration crosses cut in the top.

Entrance to the eastern range of buildings is gained from the Lower Courtyard by the fourteenth-century **Porch,** of rather later date than the Great Hall and Kitchens to which it gives admittance. It has a stone bench on either side, the left one supporting a Roman altar found in the meadows between Haddon and Bakewell. A short passage leads from the porch to a double door immediately opposite which gives access to the Upper Courtyard (*not shown to visitors*).

The **Kitchen** is approached by a dark passage and is a large, low room, containing many interesting relics of the past. The room is of about the same period as the Banqueting Hall, but the roof was possibly lowered and altered when the upper storeys of the north wing were added at a later date. Still to be seen are the original chopping-block, water troughs and oak dressers, and the huge fireplace for roasting. In the room next to the kitchen are the old bake-ovens and beyond that is the place where the carcases of animals were cut up.

The **Banqueting Hall** is one of the oldest parts of Haddon, having been built early in the fourteenth century, and it still retains much of its ancient character, with the original oak entrance screen hiding the passage beneath the Minstrels' Gallery, and with the dais for the high table at the upper end. The gallery which runs along the east side of the hall is of later date and was constructed to make a convenient approach from the Drawing Room to the rooms on the upper floors of the northern range of buildings. In 1923-5 the Banqueting Hall was entirely re-roofed, though in a seventeenth-century style in keeping with the rest of the mansion. The high table on the dais dates from about 1400 and was for the use of the family and guests. On the wall above hangs a very fine piece of English tapestry, said to have been given to one of the Vernon family by Henry VIII. The Royal Arms may be seen in the centre of the panel, while in each of the four corners is a royal coat surrounded by a garter. One authority suggests that it is of the period of Edward IV (1460-70). The huge fireplace is of a later date than the Hall itself. The original means of heating would have been a brazier, the smoke finding its way out through an opening in the roof.

The **Dining Room** is of the Tudor period and the beams of the ceiling are still covered with their original paint, dating from about 1490. The whole ceiling is probably the work of Sir Henry Vernon (1467-1515), who married the daughter of the Earl of Shrewsbury, and the badge of her house, the Talbot dog, alternates with the Tudor rose in most of the panels. Near the fireplace, however, may be seen the Vernon and Dymock Coats of Arms. The wall panelling was added by Sir George Vernon (1517-67). Above the fireplace is the motto of the Vernons, "*Drede God and Honor the King,*" and over this are panels showing a small shield with the feathers of the Prince of Wales (afterwards Edward VI), the Royal Arms of England and the shield of the Vernons. All the woodwork, including the floor, which is the original one, is oak.

The **Great Chamber,** reached by a stone staircase, dates back, structurally, to the fourteenth century, though certain alterations were carried out in the seventeenth century. Of these, the very fine plaster frieze still remains. The oriel window looks out over the Upper Gardens to the broad flight of steps leading on to the Terraces and to the footbridge where John Manners traditionally waited with the horses on the night he eloped with Dorothy Vernon. A portrait reputed to be that of the heroine of the story hangs near this window. The walls are hung with four panels of seventeenth-century Verdure Tapestry from Paris.

Beneath this wing lies part of the Norman precinct wall, and upon this in the late fourteenth century a long half-timbered room was built. Subsequently this was converted into a Library and Smoking Room. *It should be noted that these rooms are not shown to the public.*

The steps to the **Long Gallery** are said to have been cut from the root of a single oak-tree grown in Haddon Park, and the whole floor from the tree itself. Some of the boards are as much as 22 inches in breadth. Sir George Vernon probably began the work in the Long Gallery, but the panelling and ceiling are the work of Sir John Manners (d. 1611). The room is 110 feet 6 inches long and 17 feet 4 inches broad, and panelled throughout. The plain work is oak and the carved work walnut, while the dark stripes in the columns are bog oak. The panelling is more elaborate than that in any other room in the Hall and reflects the influence of the Renaissance. In the frieze the Manners' Shield, surmounted by a peacock, and the Vernon Shield, surmounted by a boar's head, as well as a Rose and Thistle design, can be seen. The windows contain many of the original panes, often of darker glass. The ceiling is divided into designs of various shapes and also shows the shields of Vernon and Manners. Over the fireplace is a picture, painted by Rex Whistler in 1933, incorporating a strip of sixteenth-century picture of the Hall in such a manner that the join is scarcely visible. The oak vestment chest dates from the fourteenth century.

The panelled **Ante-Room,** belonging to the eastern range of buildings, is older than the Long Gallery. It contains the door through which Dorothy Vernon is supposed to have eloped.

The **State Bedroom,** or Orange Room, is also of earlier date than the Long Gallery, being of fifteenth-century construction, though the ceiling and plaster frieze are a later addition and may have been the work of Sir John Manners. The tapestries represent hunting scenes and were probably woven in Brussels about 1500. Over the fireplace is a plaster relief representing Orpheus charming all Nature and embodying the Manners' peacock.

The Gardens

On leaving the Hall by Dorothy Vernon's Door the visitor will find himself on a Terrace with a rose garden at one end and a bowling green at the other. This terrace and the top terrace are separated from the Upper Garden by a long stone balustrade, broken by a flight of steps which leads down to the lower level. From this point there is a delightful view of the South Front of the

Hall. Between the Upper and Lower Gardens is a fine gate which dates back to the reign of Charles II. The River Wye flows in a curve round this side of Haddon and a steep flight of steps near the Chapel leads down to " Dorothy's Bridge," as well as to the terraces of the Lower Garden. Here the huge buttresses, with their flower-filled crevices, form a striking contrast to the light and graceful balustrade of the Bowling Green Terrace and steps.

The road from Bakewell past Haddon Hall continues to—

Rowsley

a charming little village of grey stone cottages beloved of anglers and artists. It stands on a tongue of land at the confluence of the Derwent and the Wye; the " waters-meet " is a pretty spot. There is a small church, erected in 1855, in the Norman style. At the eastern end of the north aisle there is a mortuary chapel containing the altar-tomb of the first Lady John Manners and her infant child, with beautifully sculptured recumbent figures, the work of Calder Marshall. The *Peacock Hotel* was originally a manor-house, built in 1652.

Rowsley to Bakewell by the Old Road.—This is the pleasantest route (3½ miles) for walkers. The track, in its higher parts a grass one, strikes northwards close to the *Peacock* at Rowsley, and, going under the railway, passes the prettily placed little church. Then it winds upwards and reaches three gates, beyond which, after passing through the left-hand one, it continues through a wood on a comparative level to a *col* from which there is a beautiful view both in front and behind. The *col* separates two short valleys, one opening on to Rowsley, the other on to Bakewell. Our track does not cross the *col*, but drops along the right-hand side of the latter valley, and the rest of the way is quite obvious.

Rowsley to Chatsworth.—The road lies due north from Little Rowsley (beyond the railway station), alongside the Derwent (a footpath starting direct from Rowsley follows the river more closely). A mile and a half onward is **Beeley,** an ancient and somewhat smaller village than Rowsley. It is noted for the grindstones made from the local hard grit. The Church contains a Norman round-headed doorway, believed to have been removed from an earlier church. The embattled tower is sixteenth-century work.

About half a mile beyond the village Chatsworth Park is entered at Beeley Lodge. The House is a mile from the lodge, or 3 miles from Rowsley. For the continuation by road to Edensor and Baslow, *see* p. 95.

CHATSWORTH

(**Access.**—*See* p. 79. **Admission.**—The Gardens are open during the period April to October: Monday to Friday 11.30-4-30, Saturday and Sunday 2-6, Good Friday and Bank Holidays 11.30-6. The House is open during the same period: Wednesday, Thursday and Friday, 11.30-4, Saturday and Sunday 2-5.30, Good Fridays and Bank Holidays and Tuesdays following, 11.30-5.30. There are admission charges. Visitors follow a marked route round the House.)

The Chatsworth estate was purchased in the sixteenth century by Sir William Cavendish, whose son by Elizabeth Hardwick (afterwards Countess of Shrewsbury) was created in 1618 Earl of Devonshire. It has since been the principal country seat of the Cavendish family. The original house, a quadrangular building with turrets curiously disposed about it, was begun by Sir William, and after his death in 1557 completed by his widow. In 1570 and again in 1573 it was the prison of Mary, Queen of Scots. A bedroom in the present house, above the Painted Hall, is still known by her name, but there is no foundation for the legend that, when the old hall was pulled down (1688-89) this room was preserved, by erecting a scaffold beneath it, and incorporated in the new building. Her imprisonment at Chatsworth is also commemorated in the name of **Queen Mary's Bower,** a square stone structure between the house and the river (built round an ancient earthwork guarding the ford), to which she is traditionally supposed to have resorted. During the Civil Wars the old house was occupied in turn by both parties as a fortress.

The present building, with the exception of the north wing, was begun in 1687 by the fourth Earl of Devonshire, created Duke (1694) in recognition of his services during the Revolution. Kennet tells us that the Earl's original intention was to rebuild the south side only (completed 1693). If it was so, he very soon changed his mind, for the demolition of the old hall, on the inner side of the east wing, was begun in the summer of 1688, and there are items in the accounts from which we may infer that it was already contemplated in the preceding December. The whole of the present house, however, was built mainly on the foundations and followed the lines of the Elizabethan building, a fact which is in itself perhaps suggestive of a gradual enlarging of the Earl's ideas as the work proceeded, rather than of a comprehensive plan adopted at the outset; and the want of system in the rebuilding (e.g. the outer side of the east wing was not begun until the inner side was almost finished, and the elaborate terrace-wall within a few feet of the west front was completed at least a year before the demolition of the west wing began) may also be reckoned an argument in support of Kennet's assertion. The west and the north sides were completed in 1702 and 1707 respectively. Within twenty years of the commencement of the rebuilding, not a stone of the Elizabethan structure was to be seen.

William Talman designed the South and East fronts, and Thomas Archer was probably responsible for the North front façade. A valuation of the building (so far as it had proceeded) was carried out in 1692 by Sir Christopher Wren, from which it has been concluded, but probably without good reason, that he assisted Talman in his designs. Among those engaged in the decoration were Verrio, Laguerre, Ricard and Sir James Thornhill, who between them painted the ceilings; the wood-carvers, Thomas Young, William Davis and Joel Lobb; Samuel Watson, a native of Heanor, who did a great quantity of carving, both in wood and stone; the sculptors Cibber, Nadauld and Nost; and Tijou, the French smith, who designed and executed the superb ironwork of the Great Stairs. It is characteristic of the period that this famous craftsman also helped the local smiths in the manufacture of nails, bolts, clamps, hinges, and such other humble accessories to the structure of the house. For the belief, already current in Walpole's time, that any part of the wood-carving was the work of Grinling Gibbons there is no foundation whatever.

The long north extension, in which are situated the modern Dining Room, Sculpture Gallery, Orangery and Theatre, was built by the sixth Duke (1820-27) to the designs of Sir Jeffry Wyatville. This building with its belvedere dominates the approach to the house through the north forecourt.

The unimposing **Sub-Hall** through which we enter was never intended for the purpose which it now serves. Until the middle of the eighteenth century it was the kitchen, the main entrance being on the west front. Here the approach was inconvenient, for coaches could advance no farther than the foot of the steps; and shortly before 1767 (the year in which Paine, the architect of the new stables and of the bridge over the Derwent, published his plans) the old stables and offices which filled the fore-court were cleared to open an approach on the north.

Over the chimney-pieces on either side of the Sub-Hall are Landseer's "Bolton Abbey in the Olden time" and Carlo Maratta's "Diana and her Nymphs" with landscape by Gaspar Poussin. Notable among the sculptures here are the Head of Alexander the Great (on newel of stairs, right), reckoned the finest of the extant antique copies of the original by Leochares, and the Roman portrait-group of a mother with her daughter of the first century A.D.

From the Sub-Hall we pass through the North Sub-Corridor to—

The Painted Hall

sixty feet in length, twenty-seven wide, and two storeys in height. Through the arch above the stone stairs at the south end may be seen Tijou's staircase (1689) ascending to the State Rooms. The oak stairs at the north end were built by Wyatville for the sixth Duke (1824). The gilt ironwork on the gallery and the lower flight of stone stairs was copied from Tijou's designs when this flight was rebuilt in 1912. The paintings on the walls and ceiling, depicting the life, death and apotheosis of Julius Caesar, are by Laguerre. Visible through the windows across the court is the old main entrance already mentioned. Over the chimney-piece of Derbyshire marble is a Latin inscription, which may be translated:—

"These dear ancestral halls, begun in the year of English freedom 1688, were inherited by William Spencer Duke of Devonshire in 1811, and completed in the year of sorrow 1840."

(In the latter year died Blanche, wife of the Earl of Burlington, afterwards seventh Duke of Devonshire. The sixth Duke was a Whig, and liked to think of Chatsworth as having been begun in the year of the Revolution: but in fact it was begun the year before.)

We next pass through the **Grotto** under the stairs (notice the beautiful fountain figuring Diana or Venus at the bath; the festoons of flowers in Roche Abbey stone; and the fine ceiling carved with the insignia of the Garter) to the **South Sub-Corridor.** Here the most prominent objects are a barge, given to the sixth Duke by the Sultan of Turkey, and cabinets containing Crown Derby and other fine china. At the end of the corridor is the **Chapel,** a finely proportioned room, unaltered except in minor details since its completion in 1692. The altar-piece, of alabaster and black marble from local quarries, with flanking figures of Faith and Justice, is traditionally attributed to Cibber; but it now seems almost certain that the figures alone were his work and that the altar-piece itself was designed and executed by Watson, who also appears to have been responsible for the wood-carving. The painting over the altar ("The incredulity of St. Thomas "), is by Verrio, and the frescoes on the north wall ("Christ healing the sick ") and on the ceiling ("The Ascension ") are by Laguerre. The carving in lime-tree on panels of cedar-wood, and the cherubs, flowers and birds above the gallery, executed in the style of Grinling Gibbons, are of especial beauty.

Leaving the Chapel, visitors enter the west sub-corridor, and pass thence up the **West Stairs** to the top storey. The ironwork on these stairs, often attributed to Tijou (of whom it is not unworthy), was executed, though not designed, by John Gardom, the local smith. In the gallery at the head of the stairs, and in that opening out of it on the south wing, is now arranged in chronological order a series of family portraits, many brought from Hardwick in 1926; prominent among these are the portraits of the ninth Duke by de Laszlo and of the present Duchess by Annigoni. The tapestries in the South Gallery (Mortlake, about 1645) were also moved from Hardwick in the same year.

A narrow lobby at the angle of the two galleries leads to the **State China Closet** which now contains a series of interesting paintings as well as fine china. These include works by Matsys, Bruyn, Ostade, and Berchem.

Here we enter—

The State Rooms

a suite of five apartments occupying the whole of the length of the south front. Built when decorative craftsmanship was at its best, they must in their original aspect have formed one of the finest suites in the kingdom. Unfortunately, however, they were drastically altered at a time (1820-40) when craftsmanship was at a very different level, and when little respect was paid to the achievements of the period in which they were built. Much of the splendid carving which adorned their wainscot panels was then destroyed, and their tapestry hangings removed to Hardwick. The walls of the Bedroom and the Music Room were covered with stamped leather, showing at frequent intervals along its frieze—lest we forget the perpetrator of the outrage—the bust, coronet and cypher of the sixth Duke. Only the last, the largest, and the noblest of the suite —the Great Chamber, or State Dining Room—remains unaltered, as in the first Duke's day

The State Rooms are filled with treasures, of which only a few can be noticed here:—

Dressing Room. The magnificent silver chandelier reveals its own date, 1694. Those who have eyes to see will discover evidence that the smith was actually at work upon it when the dukedom was created. Groups of china plates decorate the walls.

Bedroom. The two large mirrors are remarkable as being English glass. They shew the arms of the first Duke, with those of his wife, and were made by John Gumley in 1703. George II died in the silk-hung fourposter bed, which came to Chatsworth as the perquisite of the fourth Duke.

Music Room. On the inner door, facing the windows, is Vandervaart's famous violin, familiar to generations of visitors, but originally at Devonshire House. Here are the Coronation Chairs of George II and his Queen, in the style and perhaps by the hand of Chippendale himself. The table has a top of Siberian malachite and was presented to the sixth Duke by the Tsar Nicholas I.

Drawing Room. The tapestries here were woven at Mortlake in the seventeenth century, while the chests were made from the panels of Coromandel lacquer with which the first Duke originally decorated the walls of the Dressing Room.

Dining Room. This, the largest of the State Rooms survives in its original state, with its panelling and carving intact. Much of the gilt furniture was designed by William Kent and was brought from Chiswick Villa.

Leaving the State Rooms we descend to the Painted Hall, by the Great Stairs, with ironwork by Tijou, and ascend the **Oak Stairs** into the **Ante-Library.** From this room a view is obtained of the **Library** itself which contains many items of great rarity and importance, as well as a large collection of early drawings and prints by the old masters. Passing through the sixth Duke's **Dining Room,** with fine portraits by Van Dyck, and a table laid with services of china and silver, we enter the **Sculpture Gallery.** Here are many examples of the work of Canova, Thorwaldsen and other artists so popular a hundred years ago. The finest are the recumbent Endymion, the huge bust of Napoleon, and the seated figure of his mother, all by Canova. Today the Gallery has become a convenient place for the display of fine paintings, books, manuscripts etc. from the collection. Notice especially Rembrandt's famous portrait of an Oriental, Henry VIII's boxwood Rosary, with its designs by Holbein, and his father's autographed MS Prayer Book. The tapestries are from a set, " The Loves of Jupiter " woven at Brussels about 1690.

From the Sculpture Gallery we pass through the **Orangery,** with its sales counter, to—

The Gardens

These, originally laid out in the formal French style, were remodelled in the landscape style, first by the fourth Duke, in the mid-eighteenth century, then by the sixth Duke (1820-40), under the direction of Sir Joseph Paxton, who introduced a scheme of rockwork and landscape in keeping with the romantic notions then in vogue. Certain features of the old gardens, however, are preserved, e.g. the Greenhouse and the Cascade, though the Greenhouse has been moved from its original position and rebuilt. Another reminder of the old gardens is the famous Willow-Tree Fountain (cast in 1692; recast, or replaced, early in the nineteenth century) whose waters, controlled by a hidden tap, were the source of much entertainment in days when practical jokes were still fashionable. The Great Glasshouse, built by Paxton in 1836-40, and used by him as the basis of his design for the Crystal Palace, was demolished in 1920. Its stone foundations now enclose a formal garden and maze.

On the south front are the **Canal Pond,** with a fountain capable of throwing a jet of water 290 feet into the air, and the **Sea-Horse Fountain,** carved by Cibber. The southern portion of the terrace-wall is the sole remaining feature of the Elizabethan garden. Today the West Front Garden and the South Lawn are private to the Duke and Duchess and their guests.

Edensor

This pretty " model " village was laid out by Paxton and the Derby architect, Robertson, for the sixth Duke of Devonshire and is inhabited by Chatsworth estate employees.

The Church, designed by Sir Gilbert Scott, replaced an older building, but the Norman south porch, four aisle arches and some window tracery have been preserved in the present building. Chief interest, however, centres in the monuments. South of the choir is the Cavendish Chapel, with a grimly designed monument in memory of Henry and William, the two sons of the celebrated Elizabeth, Countess of Shrewsbury—" Bess of Hardwick," one of the richest women in the reign of Elizabeth. She was married four times, obtaining a large accession of wealth at each marriage, and leaving children only by her second husband, Sir William Cavendish. Their second son was eventually created first Earl of Devonshire (d. 1625). The east window of this chapel commemorates Lord Frederick Cavendish, who went out to Ireland as Chief Secretary in 1882 and was murdered in Phoenix Park, Dublin, within twelve hours of his arrival.

At the west end of the south aisle is a memorial to Sir Joseph Paxton, who designed the Crystal Palace, London, the great Glass House at Chatsworth, and had a career that was distinguished in many other directions. Few will regard, unmoved, the War Memorials in the north aisle. Of note is the Beton brass, a memorial to John Beton, Controller to Mary, Queen of Scots. He died at Chatsworth during her imprisonment here.

Half a mile beyond Edensor the road forks. The left branch divides again in 1½ miles, where the left arm descends to Bakewell, the right goes on to the Buxton road at Ashford (p. 80).

The right branch drops down to the Derwent Valley again to reach, about a mile on—

Baslow

a pretty village, charmingly situated on the eastern bank of the *Derwent*. Note the lovely three-arched bridge. The **Parish Church,** dedicated to St. Anne, on the bank of the river, has a low fourteenth-century tower, surmounted by a broach spire. There are some interesting monuments within the church, and an ancient " dog whip " to keep animals in order during the service.

Less than three-quarters of a mile east of Baslow, where the Chesterfield and Sheffield roads divide, is the northern entrance to Chatsworth Park at Park Lodge. The house is 1½ miles from the entrance gate.

Buses run from Baslow to Matlock, Buxton and Chesterfield, Sheffield and Bakewell.

Haddon Hall from the Fields (*J Salmon*)

Chatsworth House (*J Salmon*)

South Parade, Matlock (*J. Salmon*)

The Square, Matlock (*J. Salmon*)

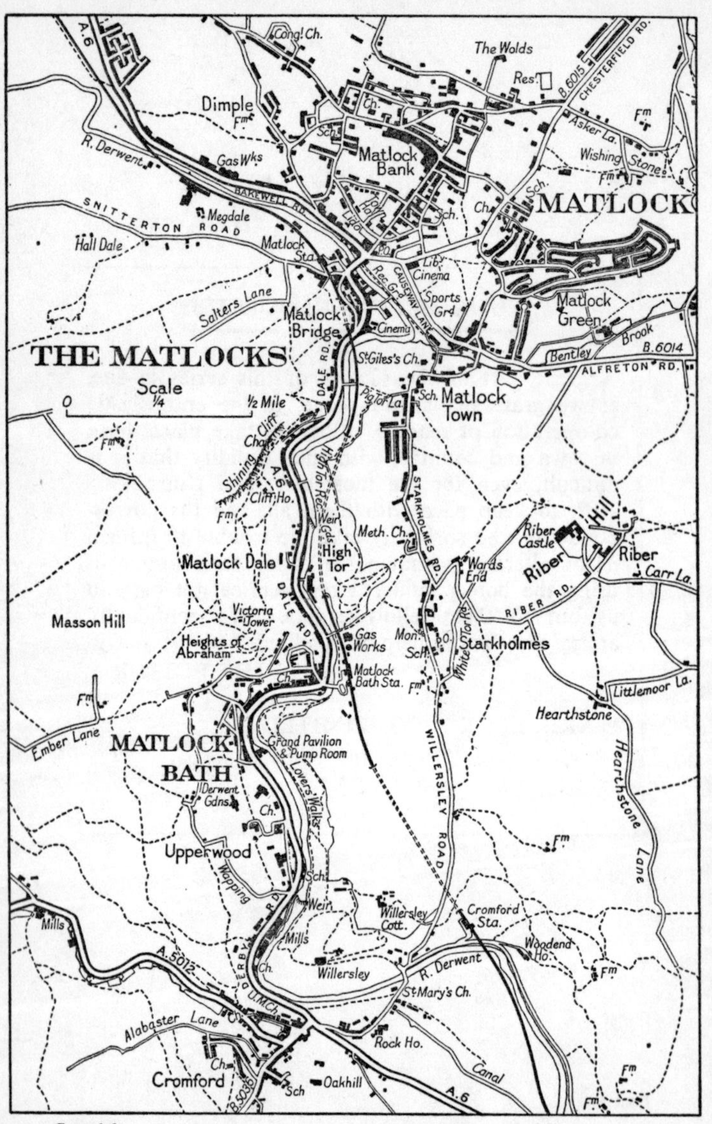
A.6
Cong! Ch.
The Wolds
B.6015
CHESTERFIELD RD.
Dimple
Fm
Res.
Fm
R. Derwent
Gas Wks
Matlock Bank
Ch.
Asker La.
Sch.
Wishing Stone
Fm
SNITTERTON ROAD
BAKEWELL RD.
Town Hall
Sch.
Ch.
MATLOCK
Megdale
Matlock Sta.
P.O.
Hall Dale
Rec. Grd
Lib.
Cinema
Matlock Green
Salters Lane
CAUSEWAY LANE
Sports Grd
Matlock Bridge
Bentley Brook
THE MATLOCKS
Cinema
B.6014
ALFRETON RD.
Scale
St. Giles's Ch.
0   ¼   ½ Mile
DALE RD.
Pig Tor La.
Sch. Matlock Town
Cliff
Chalet
Fm
Shining
A.6
High Tor Rec. Gds
STARKHOLMES RD.
Cliff Ho.
Fm
Weir
Meth. Ch.
Riber Castle
Riber Hill
Matlock Dale
High Tor
Wards End
Riber
Carr La.
Masson Hill
Victoria Tower
DALE RD.
Gas Works
Mon. Sch.
P.O.
RIBER RD.
Heights of Abraham
Ch.
Matlock Bath Sta.
White Tor Rd.
Starkholmes
Fm
Fm
Littlemoor La.
Ember Lane
Hearthstone
MATLOCK BATH
Grand Pavilion & Pump Room
WILLERSLEY ROAD
Hearthstone Lane
Derwent Gdns
Lovers' Walks
Ch.
Fm
Upperwood
Wapping
DERBY RD.
Sch.
Weir
Willersley Cott.
Cromford Sta.
Mills
Woodend Ho.
Mills
Fm
A.5012
Ch.
Willersley
R. Derwent
B.5036
DERBY ROAD
U.M.Ch.
St. Mary's Ch.
Canal
Alabaster Lane
Rock Ho.
A.6
Cromford
Ch.
Sch.
Oakhill
Fm

MATLOCK

The Peak District is a land of surprises, and Matlock is one of the best of them. The approaches from north and south are through lovely scenery, but the wide green valleys give no hint of the sudden transformation to the narrow gorge in which Matlock Bath, together with the road, the river and the railway, manages to squeeze. Those approaching from Chesterfield have an even stranger experience, for at a distance of only a few miles one has a prospect of wide-spreading uplands: there is not the slightest hint of the Matlock gorge, and until one begins to descend the hill even the more open Matlock Bridge and Bank are not seen. Nestling mainly in the dale, sheltered on all sides by hills, its climate is mild and congenial.

While Matlock continues to be the favoured resort of large numbers of day visitors from the busy industrial areas around, it is becoming increasingly recognized as an excellent centre from which to explore the southern part of the Peak District.

Access.—Matlock is on the main line from London (St. Pancras) *viâ* Derby to Manchester.

Banks.—*Midland*, Matlock; *Lloyds*, Cromford; *Westminster*, Matlock, Matlock Bank, Matlock Bath, Bonsall and Darley Dale; *Williams Deacon's*, Matlock and Darley Dale; *Derby Trustee Savings Bank*, Matlock; *C.W.S.*, Smedley Street, Matlock.

Bus and Coach Services.—Local services to all parts of the area. Bus station in Bakewell Road, Matlock. Buses run to Derby; Rowsley, Chatsworth Park Gates and Baslow; Haddon Hall, Bakewell and Buxton; Chesterfield; Manchester and Ashbourne.

Car Parking Places.—The Pavilion, Matlock Bath; Artist's Corner, Matlock Dale; Station Road, Matlock Bridge; Bakewell Road, adjoining Bus Station.

Churches and Chapels.—

Church of England: St. Giles', Matlock Town; *All Saints',* Matlock Bank; *St. John's,* Matlock Dale; *Holy Trinity,* Matlock Bath; *St. James's,* Bonsall; *St. Mary's,* Cromford; *St. Mark's,* Cromford; *St. Helen's,* Darley Dale; *Hackney Mission Church,* Hackney; *St. Mary's,* South Darley; and *Holy Trinity,* Tansley.

Roman Catholic: St. Joseph's, Bank Road.

Methodist: Trinity, Bank Road; Matlock Bank, Bank Road; Imperial Road; Starkholmes; and Matlock Moor: at Cromford (Via. Gellia; and Mount Tabor): at North Darley (Dale Road North; Darley Hillside; Hackney Lane; and Chatsworth Road, Little Rowsley): at South Darley (Oakerside; and Wensley); at Matlock Bath (The Parade); and Tansley (Brunswick).

Congregational: at Matlock (Chesterfield Road); and at Farley (Smedley Street West).

Wesleyan: at Dale Road North, Darley Dale and at The Dale, Bonsall.

Baptist: at Yeoman Street, Bonsall.

Non-denominational services are held at Mary Dobson Memorial Hall, Matlock, Torside Gospel Hall, and at " The Assembly of God," High Street, Bonsall.

Clubs.—*Conservative Club,* Dale Road; *Liberal* (non-political), Bank Road; *United Services,* Crown Square. Other clubs include *Rotary, Inner Wheel, Round Table, Ladies Circle, Townswomen's Guild,* etc.

Distances by Road,—From Matlock Bridge to Ashbourne, 14 miles; Bakewell, 8; Buxton, 20; Chesterfield, 10; Derby, 18; London, 143; Manchester, 46; Sheffield, 22.

Hotels.—*See* pp. 10–12.

Library.—Branch of County Library at Steep Turnpike, Matlock. Open 10–7; Sats., 10–5. Other branches at the Pavilion, Matlock Bath (Mondays and Fridays), and Whitworth Institute, Darley Dale (Tuesdays and Fridays).

Local Government.—The local government of Matlock is vested in an Urban District Council. The district includes Matlock Town, Bridge, Bank and Bath, with the outlying districts of Scarthin, Starkholmes and Riber, the former parishes Tansley and Cromford, North and South Darley and Bonsall, which until 1934 formed separate Urban Districts. The Council Offices are at the Town Hall in Bank Road, Matlock.

Market Days.—Tuesdays and Fridays, in Bakewell Road, Matlock.

Newspapers.—The local newspapers are the *Derby Evening Telegraph,* published every evening; the *Derbyshire Times* on Fridays; and on Saturdays the *High Peak News,* the *Matlock Mercury* and *West Derbyshire News.*

Population,—18,920.

Post Offices.—The Head Office is in Bank Road, Matlock. There are sub-offices at Matlock Bath, Cromford, etc.

Sports and Pastimes

Boating.—Rowing boats and motor boats from Derwent landing stage, adjoining the Grand Pavilion, Matlock Bath. Scooter boats on the boating lake at Hall Leys, Matlock.

Bowls.—At Hall Leys, Matlock.

Cricket.—On Causeway Lane ground and at Darley Bridge.

Fishing.—Trout and coarse fishing available. Apply *Matlock Angling Club* for particulars.

Golf.—The Matlock Golf Club has an 18-hole course on Matlock Moor. Miniature golf on the Hall Leys.

Riding.—At Darley Dale.

Swimming.—Open air Lido and enclosed pool at Bank Road, Matlock. Open air swimming pool at the New Bath Hotel, open to non-residents.

Tennis.—Courts at Hall Leys, 2*s.* per hour; and at New Bath Hotel.

Entertainments

Children's Corner.—Paddling pool, miniature railway, swings, etc. at Hall Leys. Miniature railway and amusement ground in Derwent Gardens.

Cinema.—*The Ritz*, Causeway Lane. The *Palace* in Dale Road is now used for Bingo.

Dancing.—At Grand Pavilion, Matlock Bath.

Music.—Festival in June at Matlock Bath. Band performances Sundays and holidays.

Venetian Fete.—In September; illuminations, fireworks, and decorated boats on the Derwent.

THE MATLOCKS

The Matlocks comprise Matlock, Matlock Bath, North and South Darley, Tansley, Bonsall and Cromford, united under the same local authority, the Matlock U.D.C. **Matlock Bath,** perhaps the prettiest and most popular, lies at the southern end of Matlock Dale, on the west bank of the Derwent. **Matlock** is about one and a half miles north of Matlock Bath and east of the river.

The Annals of the Matlocks

are neither full nor particularly interesting, and would have practically no link with ancient days had not the Romans been attracted to the neighbourhood by the rich lead mines. From time to time there have been discovered pigs of lead bearing Latin inscriptions: these and other ancient mining relics are in the Derby Museum (*see* p. 136) and are particularly interesting to the expert.

In 1894 a farm labourer dug up in the neighbourhood a pig of lead weighing 175 pounds. On it was a well-preserved inscription, reading:—" P(UBLI) RUBRI ABASCANTI METALLI LVTVDARES (IS) " i.e., " (from the works of) of P. Rubrius Abascantus of the Latudarian mines."

The lead mines were worked under quaint and ancient rules as to access, working and ownership of the mineral, administered by the Barmote Court, which still meets regularly, though little lead is mined today. More probably, miners seen in the old galleries are seeking fluorspar, a mineral used in the steel and other industries.

It was in the seventeenth century that the virtues of the mineral waters and the glory of the rock scenery began to attract visitors to Matlock, and the bath established in the loveliest part of the Dale gave its name to what has now become, among visitors, the most popular part of the Matlocks. Later, the district witnessed the perfecting of Arkwright's spinning and carding machines, and in more recent years the opening of hydropathic establishments gave a further great impetus to the prosperity of the neighbourhood. Nowadays there are no Curative Bath establishments, as at Buxton, but Matlock is popular both as a place to visit for a few hours and as a centre from which to explore Derbyshire.

MATLOCK BATH

Matlock Bath consists mainly of a single long street which with the railway and the river almost fill the bottom of the steep-sided Matlock Dale. Here and there shops and dwelling-houses have managed to find a footing, and behind them hotels and houses peep out from among the trees, many of them in positions which look almost inaccessible. East of the river the cliffs are clothed with trees, and on either bank are pleasant walks and gardens, well provided with seats affording delightful views.

The Grand Pavilion

The Grand Pavilion is under the control of the Matlock Bath Attractions Committee, who hold dances here throughout the year. In June there is a well-supported Music Festival and in July the contest for the title of Miss Derbyshire. Adjoining is a café formerly known as the Pump Room—a reminder that it was—

The Thermal Springs

first used in 1698, which brought prosperity to the district and gave to this particular Matlock its distinguishing name of Bath.

The following is a recent **Analysis** of the thermal springs—

	Grains per gallon	Parts in 1,000,000
Chloride of sodium ..	4.57	65.3
Sulphate of magnesium	9.73	139.0
Sulphate of calcium	2.04	29.2
Carbonate of calcium	14.68	209.7
Silica ..	0.71	10.1
	31.73	453.3
Organic matter, traces of ..		
Alumina, minute traces of ..		
Potassium, lithium, and strontium	1.03	14.7
Total dry residue ..	32.76	468.0

An authority on the subject thus describes the thermal springs:— " A weak medicinal water efficacious in colic, consumption, gout, chronic rheumatism, and cutaneous cases . . . temperate " —the temperature is sixty-eight degrees Fahrenheit, constant—" and lighter than common water. When drunk freely it has proved beneficial in dyspeptic and nephritic cases." The thermal spring is not purely medicinal, but can be used also as an ordinary beverage.

To its daily consumption many of the old inhabitants ascribe their good health and longevity. The thermal water is laid on to many houses in addition to the town supply of soft water.

Near the Pavilion is the landing stage where motor and rowing boats may be hired, a pleasure ground, a thermal water fountain, a well-stocked fish pond, and the **Petrifying Wells.** The water, soaking through the rocks, becomes charged with carbonic acid, which dissolves the limestone through which it passes. When the lime-laden water emerges into the open some of the carbonic acid gas escapes. Unable to hold in solution the whole of the lime, the water throws off the excess upon anything it touches, coating the object with a thick layer. Thus are formed the petrified " souvenirs," nests, eggs, bowler hats, children's toys, household utensils and other queerly selected objects. It is said that holiday visitors who have placed an object under the spray find it petrified when they return the following year.

South of the Pavilion are the **Derwent Pleasure Gardens,** well laid out and containing numerous attractions, including a miniature railway, and at the *New Bath Hotel* is an open-air thermal swimming bath, available to non-residents. Facing South Parade is **Holy Trinity Church,** a fine cruciform structure with a crocheted spire, and a reredos of Derbyshire marble. Still farther south and visible from the main road near Cromford is **Willersley Castle.** It was built in 1788 by Sir Richard Arkwright, and until recent years the seat of the Arkwright family. It is now a guest-house of the Methodist Guild.

Sir Richard Arkwright, the pioneer of one of the most important of British industries, was born in 1732, the youngest of thirteen children. Poorly educated, he began life as a barber, increasing his humble profits by selling hair and hair restorers. His home being in the cotton-spinning district of Lancashire, his attention was naturally drawn to that industry and to the attempts made to improve it, but he was nearly forty years of age before he entirely devoted himself to the subject. More fortunate than most inventors, he amassed great wealth by his mechanical genius, adding as well to the demand for labour and to the comfort of the civilized world. His great and lasting success was a completion of Hargreave's spinning jenny, consisting of a frame by which could be spun a vast number of threads of any degree of fineness or hardness, leaving the minder merely to feed the machine with cotton.

Sir Richard Arkwright died at the age of sixty, and was buried in Cromford Church, in which is a monument to him by Chantrey.

The Masson Mills, now owned by the English Sewing Cotton Co. Ltd., are a conspicuous feature on the river just before reaching Cromford, but the old mill is nearer the Canal wharf.

Opposite the Pavilion at Matlock Bath are—

The Heights of Abraham

(The grounds are open throughout the year.)

According to local belief, the name was given by an officer who fought under General Wolfe at Quebec in 1759. Certainly the ascent brings vividly before one the difficulties of such assaults!

There is more than one approach to the Heights. The nearest, and consequently the steepest, way, is to leave the main street of Matlock Bath at the corner of *Hodgkinson's Hotel*, on the Parade. An easier, but somewhat longer, route is to turn up Holme Road, opposite the road from Matlock Bath Railway Station.

The steep climb soon provides compensating views. At each turning is one of the glorious prospects that have given to Matlock its surpassing fame—prospects varying at each viewpoint, but each rivalling the others in charm and grandeur. The lower slopes are very thickly wooded, but higher there are unobstructed views. At the highest point (about 800 feet) is the **Victoria Prospect Tower,** affording a magnificent view over the Derwent Valley and the surrounding uplands. Equally fine is the view a little farther to the west, on the side of **Masson Hill** (*see* p. 106), reached by a walk through the wood. From this wood (*see* plan of Matlock) the visitor can reach, by a field path, the main road to Matlock Bridge.

Below the Tower is the entrance to—

The Rutland Cavern

(The caves are open from Easter to end of October. Admission charge. Refreshment Room by entrance.)

The Rutland Cavern is the largest, and one of the most interesting, of the many caverns around Matlock.

The *Great Rutland Cavern* was first found when sinking a shaft from the summit of the hill during early lead-mining operations. Originally known as the " Nestor " or " Nestes " mine, it was worked by the Romans for lead between 81 and 138 A.D. Many interesting Roman relics discovered in this area can now be seen in the British Museum. Amongst these is a pig of lead found on Cromford Moor in 1777 and presented to the Museum in 1797. It weighs 126 lb., and bears the inscription IMP. CAES, HADRIANI. AVG. MET. LVT.

To the geologist and sightseer alike, the cavern presents abundant interest and plenty of thrilling experiences, for in no other place does the story of the rocks unfold itself so completely as in these ancient workings.

Cinnabar—mercuric sulphide—has recently been found in the cavern and is of particular interest as it is the first recorded occurrence in Britain of cinnabar, or indeed of any mercury mineral.

The entrance is by way of a passage into the hillside, originally cut for the purpose of lead-mining, and one soon enters the first natural chamber—the **Roman Hall**—more than seventy feet high. The displacement of rocks, snapping of strata under the strain of volcanic action and general shrinkage and disruption of the earth's crust thousands of years ago, have all played their part in forming these underground chasms. The **Old Oak Tree** is a good example of natural rock formation, while the **Nestor Grotto** is one of the largest openings found in any cave. Nearby is the famous Jacob's Wishing Well.

A licensed *Refreshment Room* adjoins the entrance.

Situated at the summit of the Heights of Abraham grounds is—

The Masson Cavern

(Open at Easter and then daily from Whitsun until end of September. Admission charge.)

This cavern was a portion of an old Roman lead mine and a visit will suit the adventurous type of visitor. Hurricane lamps are carried and there is the thrill of the underground in complete safety with experienced guides. The natural cavern is 220 feet in length, 90 feet high and varies in width from 12 to 50 feet. The sides and roof are covered with fossil shells while large dog-tooth crystals and fluorspar sparkle like gems in the dim light. The various mineral ores to be seen are an unfailing source of interest.

The exit, at the opposite side from the entrance, is not far from the summit of—

Masson Hill

the huge mass, 1,100 feet high, which forms, in conjunction with the towering heights of the High Tor on the other side of the river, the grandest feature of the Matlock scenery. The panoramic view of the Derwent Valley in one direction, and in the other of the moorlands, rocks, and dales leading towards Dovedale, is grand enough amply to reward the climber.

A little distance away is the footpath near Ember Farm to Bonsall (*see* Walk I, p. 111). The path to the south leads to the hill named the **Heights of Jacob,** and eventually to—

The Cumberland Cavern

The cavern is more directly reached from the main A6 road by turning up by Holy Trinity Church: the rest of the way is plainly indicated. The cavern is geologically of interest as exhibiting the dislocations of strata and other effects of that mighty volcanic force which upheaved these grand hills. It claims to be the " most natural " of Matlock's subterranean attractions. The cavern was discovered during the eighteenth century, when a vein of lead was being followed, and to reach it the visitor traverses some of the old mine workings. The cavern extends about 1,000 yards into the hill, and consists of numerous chambers or cavities, each bearing a fanciful name. In some of the cavities are magnificent displays of rock scenery; huge blocks lie scattered in confusion; and one mass of limestone, supposed to be about forty tons in weight, has poised itself in falling on two points of the adjoining rock. The labyrinth of galleries in this cavern would be bewildering without the help of the guide. One gallery has a remarkable roof, 114 feet long and 25 feet wide.

Eastward from the Grand Pavilion the high-road along Matlock Dale, through which the Derwent flows, with the towering heights of Masson on the one side, and on the other the woodlands and the precipitous cliff which form the river frontage of the High Tor, present a picture of rare charm. The best view is from Artists' Corner, a little farther north of High Tor, where Dale Road bends to the right.

The High Tor
(**Admission** to grounds, adults 6*d*., children 3*d*.)

The High Tor cliff, rising from a foliage-covered slope sheer to the summit, some 400 feet, gives to the hill an appearance of greater altitude than it actually possesses. There are several entrances to the grounds, the nearest to Matlock Bath being reached by the footbridge crossing the river near the station and leading to a path under the railway. Another is near Matlock old church, at the foot of the Starkholmes Road. Those who cannot climb steep paths should take the bus to Starkholmes Post Office, opposite which is an obvious and very easy approach to the High Tor grounds. This route is also probably the best for cars.

The views from the Tor are not so picturesque as the views of it, but they are very interesting—along the Dale and over the steep flank of Masson Hill in one direction; in the other Riber Castle rises beyond the straggly village of Starkholmes and to the left of it the high ground falls away to reveal the serried streets of Matlock.

Near the top of the Tor is **Fern Cave,** a deep, winding fissure, or cleft, in the rock, probably caused by shrinkage of the limestone. It owes its name to the number of ferns found within its depths. The fissure runs from one side of the hill to the other, and those who do not mind a scramble through the narrowest part—hardly 3 feet high and apt to be muddy—can go from end to end. Another fissure near the far end of the Fern Cave is known (with or without adequate reason) as the **Roman Cave.** In hot weather there is always a breeze on the High Tor, and in the Fern Cave it is delightfully cool.

Adjoining the High Tor and also overlooking the river is **Pic Tor,** or Pig Tor. Here is the Matlock War Memorial.

The main road through the dale continues to Matlock bridge; the main railway station adjoins it on the left and over the bridge is **Matlock.**

The roads leading from the bridge are northward to Bakewell, Bank Road to Matlock Bank, and Causeway Lane on  the right to the **Hall Leys Park,** beautifully laid out with flower beds, trees, shady walks and a small lake where boats may be hired. Other attractions are tennis courts, bowling greens, scenic golf course, cafés, a miniature railway and, for the children, a paddling pool, swings and see-saws. The river bank walk joins a footpath leading to Pic Tor, from where there is a fine view of Matlock and High Tor.

Matlock is continuing its development from the original quiet village (recorded in Domesday Book as *Meslach*) and is now a fair-sized township. It is well provided with shops, a cinema, a library, and an excellent Lido—all near Crown

Square, the centre of the town. The **Lido** (open from 9–8, May to September) has two swimming baths—one an outdoor pool. Both baths are kept at a temperature of approximately 70°F., and cleansed by a constant flow of water. There are modern diving boards and chutes, and an excellent café. The **Town Hall** and **General Post Office** are in the lower end of Bank Road. The large building at the top of Bank Road was for many years a well-known hydro, built by John Smedley—a hosiery manufacturer—in 1852. This with the other later establishments made Matlock famous as a hydropathic centre. It is now used for County Council Offices.

MATLOCK TOWN

From the Hall Leys Park, a path leads to—

St. Giles' Church

first built in 1130, the mother church of the whole parish, boldly seated on the edge of a steep rock, reached by the appropriately named " Stoney Way." With the exception of the fifteenth-century tower, the structure is modern, the chancel having been rebuilt in 1859, and the nave and aisles in 1871. The architecture is after the style of the fourteenth-century Decorated. The Early English font belonging to the earlier structure stands under the tower. There are finely-carved modern choir stalls and pulpit.

Other features of interest within the Church include the Woolley monuments in the transept, and the black marble slab on the west wall near the door in memory of Adam Woolley and Grace, his wife, the former dying in 1657 at the age of 100, the latter in 1669 at the age of 110. These facts are duly recorded in an inscription which concludes:

" For the purpose of recording so extraordinary but well-authenticated an instance of longevity, and long continuance in the state of wedlock, their great-great-great-great-grandson, Adam Woolley, of this parish, gentleman, caused this monument to be erected in the year 1824."

Behind the door is a glass containing a number of garlands. These were carried at the funerals of maidens: according to Cox the custom was continued until 1820.

In the churchyard is an epitaph in memory of the gentle Derbyshire maiden, Phoebe Bown, who lived on Matlock Green, and died in 1854, at the age of eighty-two.

Riber

The hamlet of Riber occupies the summit of **Riber Hill,** a prominent height to the south-east of Matlock Town, 853 feet above the sea-level. An interesting feature of the place is the **Fauna Reserve** now established in the grounds of Riber Castle. Riber Castle was originally built by John Smedley, founder of Smedley's Hydro, as his residence. Unoccupied for many years and becoming derelict, the castle and its grounds have been taken over by a group of zoologists, who are developing a Zoo specializing in British animals and birds. *Open daily throughout the year. Charge includes car park and use of picnic grounds.* Motorists are recommended to approach *viâ* Tansley and Carr Lane.

Near the Castle are some Early British remains known as the **Hirst Stones,** consisting of masses of gritstone, arranged altar-wise.

Starkholmes

is reached from Matlock Town by Side Lane or Starkholmes Road, a narrow road running southward over the eastern spur of the High Tor. Turning northward from Starkholmes at a sharp angle and by a very steep gradient is the road to Riber. A bold rock to the left of this road is one of the many **Lovers' Leaps** to be found in Derbyshire.

WALKS AROUND MATLOCK

The walks start either from Matlock Bridge, at the north end of the Dale, or from Matlock Bath.

I.—MATLOCK BATH TO BONSALL

Enter Holme Road either by the ascent from *Hodgkinson's Hotel,* or by its lower end, opposite the approach to the railway station. Beyond the entrance to the Heights of Abraham turn along a narrow track to the right, and ascend the hill by a path leading near to a farmhouse and opening out into Ember Lane, which leads direct into **Bonsall** ($1\frac{1}{4}$ miles—*see* p. 112). (The first part of this walk is very steep, and those disinclined to much exertion should go to Bonsall by bus and walk back by the Heights of Abraham.) The return may be made by the road southward to the *Pig of Lead Inn* at the foot of the Via Gellia (*see* p. 113), continuing down the valley to Cromford, at the southern end of the Dale ($2\frac{1}{2}$ miles to Matlock Bath). This is the bus route.

II.—MATLOCK BRIDGE TO MASSON HILL
AND BONSALL

A few steps beyond the *Williams Deacon's Bank* in Snitterton Road is a cart track which passes over the railway bridge. This leads through a small farmyard in about 100 yards and becomes a footpath which continues uphill across several fields. Bear to the right at forking of paths near Greenhills Farm, which should be avoided. Pass *Masson Lees Farm* on the left, climb **Masson Hill** (p. 106). (A little beyond the farm is a turning to left, leading to the Heights of Abraham and Matlock.) Still following the path across a succession of fields, and descending the slope of Masson, we soon come within sight of Bonsall, which is about 2 miles from Matlock Bridge by this route. The return may be made by the Heights of Abraham (Walk I) or by bus, through Cromford and Matlock Bath.

Bonsall

is an interesting and old village, prettily situated at the head of a limestone valley. The ceremony of well-dressing is observed here at the beginning of August. **The Church,** built

on a rock overlooking the village, was restored and enlarged in 1863, as much as possible of the ancient structure being retained. The carved rood screen is the Bonsall War Memorial. The fourteenth-century spire is surrounded by remarkable "crowns." Another point of interest is the **Market Cross,** a shaft rising from thirteen steps and surmounted by a ball dated 1671. It was restored in 1870. From above the church a lane leads to Cromford (3 miles).

III.—MATLOCK BATH TO THE VIA GELLIA

(*a*) **Via Cromford.** On reaching Cromford turn first to the right out of the Derby road, then right again at the *Greyhound Hotel* out of the Wirksworth road. Continue up the valley, and at fork of road by the *Pig a' Lead Inn*, the Via Gellia (p. 113) will be seen leading in all its beauty to the left. Buses run as far as the *Pig a' Lead* (2 miles).

(*b*) **Via Bonsall.** Take the route to Bonsall described in Walk I. On the left, just short of Bonsall Church, is a stile giving on to a path by which the Cromford road may be reached. The road is then easily found to the inn at the entrance to the Via Gellia (1¾ miles).

(*c*) **Via Bonsall and Slaley.** Those who wish to explore farther should, opposite the *Fountain Inn*, at the southern end of Bonsall, go through a stone stile and ascend the steps beyond it. These lead to a footpath to **Slaley,** with splendid views over the hilly countryside. (Alternatively, go down the Cromford road for perhaps a quarter of a mile and there take the lane to the right. It becomes a terrace with extremely good views down into the Via Gellia valley.) In Slaley take a path on the left past Slaley Hall just below the telephone box. It descends a field on the left and then at a stile branches into field-tracks. Follow the right-hand one under the wall. At the end of three more fields the path reaches the boundary-wall of the steep wooded slope of the **Via Gellia** (*see* p.

High Tor, Matlock (*J. Salmon*)

Thorpe Cloud, Dovedale (*F. Frith*)

Dove Holes, Dovedale (*F Frith*)

In Dovedale (*F Frith*)

113).   Forty yards farther, close to Dunsley Spring, go through a wooden stile on the left (the path straight on continues along the wall-side and will take you into the "Via" higher up, at Hollow-church Way).   Hence the path, short, very pretty and steep, drops into the Via Gellia about 1¼ miles above the *Pig a' Lead*.

The Via Gellia

is the Latinized name of a drive made by John Gell, of Hopton Hall, Wirksworth, along the beautiful ravine opening out on the west of the road between Cromford and Bonsall.   The highway passes through a picturesque valley with well-wooded and steeply sloping sides.   The woods and roadside meadows are now strictly preserved.   The actual Via Gellia extends for nearly two miles above the *Pig a' Lead*.   At the road-junction, the road turning back sharply to the left climbs steeply to Middleton and affords good views of the winding, wooded valley.   **Middleton** is now incorporated with Wirksworth, and extensive quarrying is carried on.   A bus connects Middleton with Matlock and Wirksworth (or walk down the lane near the Post Office).

Those who enjoy a good walk but cannot face hills might well take the bus *to* Middleton from Matlock and walk down to and through the Via Gellia to Cromford (about 3½ miles).

IV.—MATLOCK BRIDGE TO CROMFORD

The road route by way of the Dale and below the High Tor to Matlock Bath needs no directions.

An alternative walk, though more hilly, is by way of Starkholmes, east of the river (the Starkholmes bus runs to the top of the ascent).   Just above St. Giles' Church at Matlock Town (reached from Matlock Bridge by Hall Leys) turn up to the left and proceed to climb the Starkholmes Road, running southward between the High Tor and Riber to Starkholmes (p. 110).   Once the top is reached the views on the right open out, and for some way there are very interesting and lovely vistas down the Dale and across the hills on the far side.   As we descend to Cromford the views on the right close in, but the valley down towards Whatstandwell opens up.   At the foot of the hill Cromford Bridge suddenly confronts us, with the church beyond—always a picturesque corner, but especially so towards sunset. A feat of horsemanship celebrated in local legend is commemorated in a curious inscription cut in the parapet of Cromford Bridge:—

THE + LEAP OF · M^R
B: H: MARE, JUNE . 1697 .

From Matlock Bridge to Cromford by this route is about $2\frac{1}{2}$ miles.

V.—MATLOCK BATH TO WINGFIELD MANOR

From Matlock Bath to Cromford go by the main road. Cross Cromford Bridge down to the left, and take the road to the right, following the winding of the river.

Keep straight on through Lea Bridge to Holloway, in the vicinity of which the scenery is very lovely. On the right beyond the village is—

Lea Hurst

a place of national interest through having been for so long the home of Florence Nightingale. It is one of the most

beautiful spots in the district, surrounded by hills, rocks and wood, to which the silvery Derwent adds charm. The park and grounds form a prominent feature in the landscape from any of the surrounding hills. The House is built of Derbyshire gritstone with grey slate slab roofs. *It is now strictly private as a home for the elderly.* Visitors are shown house and gardens only after previous arrangement.

A little beyond Holloway is the hamlet of **Wakebridge,** and then on the left rises **Crich Stand,** which has an elevation of 942 feet above sea-level. The Tower, replacing earlier structures, was rebuilt and dedicated in 1922 as a *War Memorial* to 11,400 of the *Sherwood Foresters* (*Notts and Derby Regt.*).

The Stand may be easily reached from **Crich** and commands an impressive view.

Crich

now a small village, was once a flourishing market town. The antique houses, spacious market-place, and old-world fountain are evidences of a commercial importance which has departed. **St. Mary's Church** is built mainly in the fourteenth-century Decorated style, and took the place of an older structure of which parts remain. The chief features of interest are the octagonal spire, the two Norman arcades—one with round, the other with square capitals—the beautiful Gothic windows of the chancel—and the Norman font.

Of interest in Crich is the unique **Tramway Museum,** the only one of its kind in the country. Here may be seen, in working order, horse, steam and electric tramcars. The vehicles have been brought from all parts of the British Isles for preservation as a memorial to this once familiar form of street transport.

Turn left in the centre of Crich, along the Alfreton road. In little over a mile a track on the right leads to the picturesque ruins of—

Wingfield Manor

The house was erected in the fifteenth century. In the reign of Elizabeth I it was used as one of the prisons of Mary, Queen of Scots; the remains of the room she occupied, with its large octagonal window, still exist. It was during her imprisonment here that Anthony Babington of Dethick, four miles away, originated the unsuccessful plot for her restoration that cost him his head. (There is an inscribed slab to his memory in Crich Church.)

The habitable part is now used as a farmhouse, and the manor is open to view (see notices). Architecturally, the place is interesting as being an early specimen of a quadrangular building. Its chief features of interest are the fine gateway opening into the two courts, the lofty tower, the gable ends of the banqueting hall, and the groined crypt, one of the finest in England.

The road to the right in the village leads in half a mile to Wingfield Station, on the line between Chesterfield and Ambergate, the junction for Matlock. The distance from Matlock Bath to Wingfield Station by the route above is nearly 9 miles. There is a bus service between Wingfield and Matlock.

VI.—MATLOCK BATH TO THE BLACK ROCKS

From Cromford go up to Wirksworth road, left of the *Greyhound Hotel,* for about a quarter of a mile. Then, on the left, a path passes between a modern house and a wood, then over the High Peak Railway. Beyond, easily found but not easily reached, for the climb is a steep one, will be seen—

The Black Rocks

about 2 miles from Matlock Bath. These weather-worn heights, viewed from different standpoints, present many and strange forms, which have won for them various names in the popular fancy. The most prominent projection looks from one point like a great gun levelled threateningly towards Riber, Castle; from another position it bears a grotesque resemblance to the contour of **Punch's Nose,** by which name it is popularly called. The silly practice of carving names and initials is freely indulged here as elsewhere; but on the heights is evidence of one knife whose owner and wielder stands apart from the carving crowd as one to be forgiven. No description of the view can surpass the carver's eulogistic tribute— " Heavens, what a goodly prospect spreads around! "

The High Peak Mineral Railway, crossed on the climb to the Black Rocks, joins the Derby–Matlock line near Cromford, and is one of the most romantic structures of its kind in Britain. The line originated at a time when canals were in high favour as a means of cheap transport, and the general principles of canal engineering were adapted in laying out the railway. In the course of its route from the Cromford Canal at Cromford to the Peak Forest Canal at Whaley Bridge it climbs to a height of over 1,000 feet. To-day such climbs would be made by careful contouring or with the aid of sections of rack-and-pin working, but in those days such methods were unknown; wherefore the canal principle was used, and where a particularly stiff gradient had to be negotiated the train was hauled up or down by means of a cable (on the analogy of a canal lock). Parts of the original railway are still in use, but others have been supplanted by more modern ways.

The Black Rocks to the Via Gellia.—Those who prefer to return by a different route may do so by regaining the main road from which they crossed the fields to the Black Rocks, and turning to the left, away from Cromford. At an arch of the High Peak Railway take the turning to right, and in about half a mile turn right again to **Middleton-by-Wirksworth.** Ascend the hill through the village, and from the top will be seen the Via Gellia valley, some 600 feet below. Descend into the valley as far as the junction of three roads: that on the right leads through the Via Gellia to Cromford and Matlock Bath, about 4 miles. (Buses from the *Pig a' Lead Inn,* 2 miles away.)

The Black Rocks to Whatstandwell.—Pass under the railway bridge on the Cromford-Wirksworth road, and at once turn to the left and then to the right, past Bolehill. Wirksworth and its quarries are seen below on the right. On reaching the *Malt Shovel Inn* turn to the left and follow the increasingly lovely road down to the main road (bus route) at **Whatstandwell,** about 5 miles, where a fourteenth-century bridge crosses the Derwent. In the final stages Crich Stand with its quarry is very imposing in front. *Or* keep straight on at the *Malt Shovel,* take the left-hand road at the fork a quarter of a mile or more on, and at the T-road beyond **Alder-Wasley** turn to the left. **Shining Cliff Woods**—lovely with rhododendrons in June—are on the right as this road descends to Whatstandwell. The meadows between Shining Cliff (now in the care of the National Trust) and the river are very popular with campers. In the woods is the Shining Cliff Youth Hostel.

The lane to the right, past that to Whatstandwell, leads in less than 2 miles to **Alport Height** (National Trust), " a mere shred of wild country snipped off from the vast stretch of moorlands to the north." The highest point is over 1,000 feet above the sea and the views are really splendid. An old stone direction post dated 1710 points the way to " Ash-born," Derby and Wirksworth. The needle-like Alport Stone is a remarkable feature.

VII.—MATLOCK TO MATLOCK BATH *viâ*
MASSON FARM

From Artists' Corner in Dale Road (midway between Matlock Bath and Matlock) St. John's Road ascends sharply and leads past St. John's Church. Beyond the church the road enters a lovely wood, at the end of which is Cliff House. Here on the right is a footpath ascending alongside the wood. Pass through a stile, cross the field to another stile, enter a walk by *Masson Farm,* and go across more fields to the Heights of Abraham (p. 105). The road down to Matlock Bath needs no description.

The distance is not more than 2 miles.

A return may be made by walking up Holme Road, opposite Matlock Bath Station bridge, as far as a direction post on the right marked " Public footpath to Matlock Bridge." The path leads by the varied and picturesque rocks forming the western boundary of Matlock Dale and is interesting not only for the scenery through which it passes, but for the fine views it commands of the other side of the Dale. It comes out into Cliff Road by the right side of Cliff House.

VIII.—MATLOCK TO RIBER AND TANSLEY

From St. Giles' Parish Church at Matlock turn right along the Starkholmes Road until the secondary school is reached. Immediately to the left of the school is a direction post to *Riber, Lea* and *Holloway*. A well-defined path leads upward to the hamlet of Riber, and Riber Castle (*see* p. 110) with its new Fauna Reserve.

A rather longer, but less steep, route (especially if the bus is taken to Starkholmes Post Office) is the Starkholmes road. A hundred yards or so beyond Starkholmes Post Office take the lane forking up to the left and then keep round to the left again. On reaching some cottages turn up to the right, with increasingly good views over the High Tor towards Bonsall. In about half a mile *Riber Hall* is reached. Buses ply from here on certain days to Matlock *viâ* Tansley.

To reach **Tansley** on foot (about 1¼ miles), take the lane to the right just before arriving at Riber Hall (Carr Lane). Less than half a mile down there is a stile, left, giving access to a path over a series of fields leading into the Matlock and Tansley high-road. Alternatively, follow Carr Lane for another half mile, then turn left by Alders Lane.

IX.—RIBER TO LEA HURST AND CROMFORD

This can be made a continuation of the previous walk. Less than half a mile south-west of Riber Hall on the road to Starkholmes is *Hearthstone Lane*, its name due to the fact that to the farm was brought iron ore for smelting—fuel being provided by the now-vanished woods. Beyond Hearthstone Farm bear up to right by a rough overgrown lane and follow this over the hill-top, whence the views over Derwent Dale are very lovely. A footpath leads down through Combs Wood, the Cromford–Holloway road being entered opposite **Lea Hurst** (*see* p. 114). Cromford may be gained by turning to the left for a quarter of a mile, then left again over the river and the railway to the **Cromford Canal,** which is followed to the Wharf a little above Cromford Church, from which the Derby–Matlock high-road is just up to the left.

The distance from Riber to Cromford by this route is 4 miles.

X.—MATLOCK TO DETHICK

To Riber, as described in Walk VIII. Turn along Carr Lane for about 1¼ miles, take the road to the right, then the footpath (left) across the fields to—

Dethick

3 miles from Matlock Bridge. Here is a thirteenth-century Chapel (now the parish church), with a good sixteenth-century tower. The *Manor Farm*, close by, was the birthplace of Anthony Babington, whose Roman Catholic conspiracies against Queen Elizabeth cost him his life.

The return to Matlock Bridge (about 3½ miles) may be made by turning to the right (west), keeping left at two fork-lanes, and passing *High Leas Farm* to Hearthstone Lane; then proceeding right, along this, past *Hearthstone Farm* to meet the road between Riber (right) and Starkholmes.

XI.—MATLOCK BATH TO DETHICK

From Cromford, at the southern end of the Dale, turn down to the left over Cromford Bridge, then branch to the right, by the river. A little beyond the railway bridge cross a stile on the left to a path leading past an old limekiln to a cart-road. Enter the path opposite by a stone stile and walk uphill, bearing very slightly to right, until a stile is seen on the left opening into the cart-road known as Hearthstone Lane. Opposite this stile is another, giving access to a path leading through fields to *High Leas Farm,* beyond which branch right, then left, then right again to reach Dethick (*see* above), which is about 3½ miles from Matlock Bath by this route.

XII.—MATLOCK BRIDGE TO ASHOVER

From the west side of Matlock Bridge go past the Cinema House and along Causeway Lane, and continue through

Tansley, bearing to the left into the Clay Cross road beyond the village. Then take the second turning on the left and, disregarding the turnings to left and right, keep along the grass-covered lane by a farmhouse, over the brow of a hill, and down the tree-covered slopes of *Raven's Nest Tor.* The route now lies by some cottages, over the spar-covered hillocks of the Gregory Lead Mine, to the left of **Overton Hall,** once the property of Sir Joseph Banks, the eminent navigator and the companion of Captain Cook in his voyage round the world.

Among the many curious rocks in the neighbourhood, rising in rugged grandeur from the banks of the river, is **Robin Hood's Mark,** a huge block of stone, evidently placed in position by human hands. Near it, on the hill above Overton Hall, is a rocking-stone known as the **Turning Stone.**

Keep straight on up the hill from the Hall and find footpath and lane to the right, down the reverse slope and up the ascent into Ashover, not more than 6 miles from Matlock Bridge.

Ashover

a quiet little place, pleasantly situated amid rocky scenery, is becoming increasingly popular among visitors who look for a comparatively secluded holiday resort in a bracing region.

The **Parish Church** (All Saints), completed in 1419, is surmounted by a tower and a graceful spire. Among the interesting features of the interior are the Norman font and a beautifully carved screen. The font, probably dating from 1150, one of the few leaden ones in existence, is cylindrical in shape, and ornamented by figures of men in bas-relief. Each figure stands beneath a semicircular arch, supported by slender pillars. The fine alabaster tomb of the Babington of Dethick dates from 1518. The oak carvings are also of interest: they are the work of a modern local artist.

Half a mile east of the Church are the ivy-clad ruins of **Eastwood Old Hall,** destroyed by the cannons of the Parliamentary Army during the Civil War.

Near Ashover, at Hill Top House, is **Pan's Garden,** an educational Zoo, open daily to the public from 11 a.m. to dusk.

Ashover to Matlock (about 5 miles).—From Ashover take the road westward, passing the light railway terminus (no service: the nearest station is Wingfield—3 miles). Turn left for Kelstedge, and left again after passing the first cottages to the Matlock–Chesterfield road, then cross over to a path through "The Trossachs." Follow the winding path until it emerges into a lane, turn left uphill, cross the road at the end of the lane to a stile and take the path over the moor, being careful to avoid the left-hand path at the farther side of the plantation. On reaching a wall the path follows it for a short distance to the right and comes out into Sandy Lane, where turn left to the Matlock road, and to the right on reaching it.

XIII.—MATLOCK BRIDGE TO DARLEY MOOR

This is an interesting moorland walk, commanding extensive views. Start by the Chesterfield road and at the cross-roads about two miles out, at the top of Amber Hill, whence there is a fine prospect over the Ashover valley, turn to the left along the by-road over **Darley Moor.** In about 1½ miles take the left-hand turning at the cross-roads and, on reaching a more important road in three-quarters of a mile, beside the reservoir (on the right) known as Darley Flash Dam, turn to the left. In about half a mile is **Sydnope Hall,** now a home for old people, then come some fine views over the reach of the Derwent Valley known as Darley Dale. The road eventually reaches the outskirts of Matlock at Farley: by keeping straight ahead one comes to Smedley Street (left) and Matlock Bank. The whole round is about 8 miles.

XIV.—MATLOCK BRIDGE TO TWO DALES
(DARLEY DALE)

From the Bridge go up Bank Road, then turn left along Smedley Street and past the Church to the junction of four roads. The more pleasant route is by the right of these roads, up the hill, and by a turning to left. The path passes a quarry and eventually emerges on the hill-top, from which is a view of the upper part of Two Dales. Avoid the steep and narrow path in front, and bear to right, along a cart-track and through a gate, to a road on the left leading down into the Dale. At the bottom the path on the left is the direction of Two Dales, but the walker is advised to turn to the right along the pretty, shady road as far as the romantically situated pond, and then return by the same path and descend to **Two Dales,** which is about 4 miles from Matlock Bridge by this route. A large holiday caravan park known as "Two Dales Cara-Hols Model Park," is on the west of main road. Fully equipped caravans may be hired, or owners of caravans may rent a site.

Buses return along the main road (2¼ miles) to Matlock Bridge.

XV.—MATLOCK BRIDGE TO WENSLEY

From the west side of Matlock Bridge turn right along the Snitterton road. About 100 yards beyond Salters Lane, and on far side of *The Shaws,* is a stile beside a field gate from which a path goes through a long succession of fields to Jughole Wood. Go through the wood, cross two fields, and pass into the lower end of Lea Wood. From this, take the path leading diagonally through a field, at the top corner enter another field, and keep to path by a wall on the right. At end of wall cross a stile, and go on through two more fields to yet another stile, along a broad track leading to **Wensley Dale** and the hamlet of **Wensley** (p. 124—about 3 miles—buses to Matlock).

To return on foot take the path on the right between the rocks, down the Dale; enter a field-path up a hill and follow it to a stile in the corner, then, at the end of several fields, take the middle path to **Snitterton.** The old bull ring here has been restored in recent years. Return thence by the direct road to Matlock Bridge or alternatively turn left and in a quarter of a mile take footpath on right and follow the bank of the Derwent river to Matlock Bridge.

OTHER EXCURSIONS FROM MATLOCK

I.—TO ROWSLEY, HADDON HALL AND CHATSWORTH

Distances.—Matlock Bridge to Rowsley, 4¼ miles; Haddon Hall, 6½; Chatsworth House, 7.

From Matlock road and rail run north-westward to that portion of the Derwent Valley known as—

Darley Dale

The Dale—or at any rate that portion of it seen from the main road—is hardly so romantic as its name suggests, for as a suburb it has outgrown its famous neighbour. St. Elphin's is a widely known public school for girls. Sir Joseph Whitworth, the famous engineer, lived in Darley Dale. The area is popular with anglers (fly-fishing) and garden-lovers who can inspect the famous garden nurseries.

The old church of Darley lies away to the left of the main road, but may be seen by a short detour. Take the left-hand turning about 2 miles from Matlock Bridge and proceed for about a mile. The twelfth-century **Church** boasts a Burne-Jones window but is more widely celebrated for its wonderful yew, said to be more than two thousand years old. At the thickest part it is over 32 feet in girth and it is one of the largest trees in Britain. The earliest parts of the church are Norman, but traces of Saxon stonework have been found, indicating that there was probably a Saxon church there and stone from which was included in the present building. There are two fonts, one early Norman and the other Jacobean. There are several interesting monuments in the church, including a recumbent effigy of Sir John de Darley, which dates from early in the fourteenth century. The earliest of the eight bells in the tower was cast in 1704.

The road past the church goes on to rejoin the main road. In 1½ miles farther the routes for Haddon Hall and Chatsworth diverge. For the former turn left, under the railway and over the Derwent, to Rowsley (p. 89) and continue up the valley of the Wye. **Haddon Hall** is described on pages 83–9. For **Chatsworth** keep to the right at the junction. The route thence is given on page 89.

II.—TO WINSTER, ROWTOR ROCKS AND STANTON MOOR

Distances.—Matlock Bridge to Winster, by road all the way (or by rail or bus to Darley Dale, 2½ miles, and thence by road), 5½ miles; Rowtor Rocks, 7; Robin Hood's Stride, 8; Alport. 9¼.

Walkers will be well advised to take train or bus to Darley Dale where a detour may be made to see the venerable yew (*see* p. 123). Otherwise one keeps to the Winster road. Cross the Derwent by a four-arched bridge, and ascend through the village of **Wensley.** The name, it is said, is a corruption of the Latin *occursus,* signifying "conflict," and is due to the former existence of a fort built upon the summit by the Romans to intimidate the Britons.

At the foot of this hill the road from Matlock *viâ* Snitterton (p. 122) comes in on the left and converges with our route. The rest of the way to Winster is along the side of a pleasantly wooded valley.

Winster

is a large village, once with a considerable market, consisting of one wide street and two or three smaller ones climbing the hill on the left. In the main street is the stone *Market House* of the late seventeenth-century date, belonging to the National Trust. The village is a centre for folk dancing and is well-known for its mumming dance. A traditional pancake race is held on Shrove Tuesday each year.

Direct route from Winster to Robin Hood's Stride, 1¼ miles. Follow the Bakewell road from the west end of the village for about a mile and then take a path to the left, which climbs up a hill past a small farmstead on the right, and then doubles round the north side of the "Stride" to the table of rock which forms the summit. The two tower-shaped rocks which mark the extent of the "stride" (*see* p. 125) are conspicuous all the way.

The road from Winster to Birchover (for the Rowtor Rocks) leaves the west end of the village and bears right from the Bakewell road. (At **Elton,** less than a mile west from here, is a Youth Hostel.) Pedestrians should follow a route which begins with a short lane a few yards west of the Market House, and crosses the valley towards the village of **Birchover,** the quarries of which are seen high ahead. At the only fork, take the branch over the flagged causeway. In three-quarters of a mile it enters a lane which climbs a steep pitch to Birchover, where there are old stocks, a bull ring, and some interesting geological and archaeological relics preserved by the local society. From the top of this lane turn to the left: in a few hundred yards is reached the *Druid Inn*, through which—

Rowtor Rocks

are entered. There is nothing Druidical about them, but in shape and disposition they are even more eccentric than the average curiosities of the gritstone formation. There are well-worn passages up and down and through the midst of them, and the inevitable " rocking-stone," and, what is more, they command a beautiful view.

They have been described as " A remarkable assemblage of rocks, which extends in length between 70 and 80 yards and rises to the height of about 40 or 50 yards. Near the east end is a large block of an irregular shape, which several writers have noticed as a rocking-stone which could be shaken by the hand. Now, however, it requires the whole strength to put it in motion through having been forced from its equilibrium by the mischievous efforts of fourteen young men, who assembled for that purpose on Whit-Sunday, in the year 1799. It has been restored to its former situation, but the exact balance it once possessed is entirely destroyed. At a little distance northward is a second rocking-stone, not very dissimilar to an egg laid on one side, which may be moved by the strength of a single finger, though it is 12 feet in length and 14 in girth. More directly north is another rocking-stone, resembling the latter both in figure and facility of motion, and at the west end are seven stones piled one over another, various in size and form, but two or three very large, all of which may be shaken by the pressure of the hand; the effect being produced by the application of the hand to various parts." (*Bateman.*)

Just opposite and across the valley are the twin turrets of Robin Hood's Stride, and Cratcliffe Tor.

From the Inn the road curves down to the Alport–Winster road below Cratcliffe Tor (*see* p. 126), but good walkers can be recommended to make a detour over—

Stanton Moor

From the *Druid Inn* return up the hill, through Birchover

village. Beyond the quarries the road runs out on to **Stanton Moor,** a plateau over 900 feet above the sea commanding lovely views over the Wye and Derwent valleys. In 1934 Stanton Moor Edge was given to the National Trust.

In the words of the *Manchester Guardian*: "The beauty of the country is only one of the reasons why it has been given to the Trust; it is also of considerable archaeological interest, and for over a century archaeologists have worked on the many stone circles, round barrows, rocking-stones, altars, rock idols, and sacrificial basins which surround the property. Most of these have been attributed to the culture of the Bronze Age, between 1500 and 500 B.C., but there is also evidence of later Celtic habitation. In the nineteenth century, when archaeologists were inclined to attribute anything they could not quite understand to the Druids, there arose theories of Stanton as a Druid centre, but modern methods and knowledge have thrown suspicion on many of these theories. However, some of the monumental rock structures are still generally considered to have some connection with this mysterious cult."

On the property itself there are four of these huge rocks which have aroused curiosity—the **Cat Stone,** the **Gorse Stone,** the **Druid Stone,** and the **Heart Stone.** It is now accepted that all of them may have been made and raised to their positions by natural forces, but many bear inscriptions and the marks of human work of an early date. Near by are other more famous rocks such as the **Nine Ladies,** the **Castle Ring,** the **Nine Stones, Six Stones,** and **Andle Stone,** and many cinerary urns and other relics have also been found on the moor.

At the northern end of the ridge is the picturesque little village of **Stanton-in-the-Peak,** which, in addition to the charm of its situation on the slope of a densely-wooded hill, has an eighteenth-century Gothic-style Church and a small inn, named after a once-celebrated racehorse, *Flying Childers*. From Stanton we drop steeply to the Alport–Winster road (where turning right is gained the Matlock–Bakewell–Buxton main road and bus route), about a mile below Cratcliffe Tor.

Those who do not visit Stanton Moor on this occasion can follow the footpath leading from the *Druid Inn*; past St. Michael and All Angels Church with its beautifully carved pulpit, the work of a former vicar, on past Bradley Rocks down to the Alport–Winster road at the foot of **Cratcliffe Tor** and Robin Hood's Stride. The former consists of huge masses of disrupted gritstone, of which its summit forms quite a Cyclopean table. At the foot of its sheer part and just above a rustic farmstead is the *Hermit's Cave*, a shallow cave, walled-in and guarded by a pair of yews. Inside is a notched crucifix, the figure showing no great dilapidation, although the date of origin is possibly twelfth century.

From Cratcliffe Tor to **Robin Hood's Stride** is scarcely a stone's-throw. The "Stride" is also called *Mock Beggars Hall*, and indeed one may, with very little strain, imagine the Autolycuses of past years being deceived by the artificial appearance of its façade and turrets when they first saw them from the valley below. The stride which Robin Hood is said to have taken to get the place named after him—*i.e.* the distance from turret to turret—is perhaps 10 to 15 yards.

From the "Stride" the walker should go north-west by a path that enters the Elton–Alport road, where turn to the right.

The hamlet of **Alport** is delightfully situated at the junction of the Bradford and Lathkil rivers and makes a very useful centre for several pretty walks of moderate length. It is the very picture of an English hamlet, and is a charming place for a quiet holiday. Half a mile to the west may be seen the tower of Youlgreave Church (*see* below). The road from Alport to Haddon Hall (p. 83) runs for nearly 1½ miles along the narrow little *Dakin* valley, which opens on to the wider valley of the Wye half a mile south-east of the Hall. From this point a bus may be taken to Bakewell or Matlock, or it is a walk of about a mile to Rowsley and the railway (p. 89).

III.—TO YOULGREAVE AND ARBOR LOW

Route.—Pedestrians should take the Bakewell bus as far as the Youlgreave turning, about a mile west of Rowsley. Thence to Youlgreave is about 2½ miles, and Arbor Low a further 3½ miles. Motorists and cyclists can make this a continuation of the previous route.

Youlgreave

on the hillside above the *Bradford*, is an extensive village, with a fine **Church**, whose fifteenth-century tower is a conspicuous object from the country around. It contains several interesting monuments—amongst them a tomb and alabaster effigy, excellently preserved, of Thomas Cokayne (*d.* 1488) in the chancel, and a remarkable font, 800 years old, with a projecting stoup. There are many monuments to the Gilbert, Eyre and Thornhill families: note that on the wall at the east end of the north aisle showing a lady with her nineteen children, and beside it the little brass to Fridswide Gilbert. The glass of the east window—by Morris and designed by Burne-Jones—is notable. An annual well-dressing ceremony takes place at Youlgreave on the Saturday nearest to 24th June.

The lovely **Bradford Dale,** in the neighbourhood of Youlgreave, is one of the prettiest features of the county.

Youlgreave to Bakewell. Take road going north from the Church. In a mile it descends and crosses the Lathkil at a pretty spot, with views of Over Haddon up the valley. On regaining the heights it is worth pausing for the sake of the view over the Derwent valley, with Haddon Hall down among the trees. At the cross-roads turn to the right for Bakewell (p. 79), which is about 3½ miles from Youlgreave.

Walkers with an hour to spare are recommended to vary this route either by leaving the road where it crosses the Lathkil and taking the river-side path to the mill below Over Haddon (*see* p. 129) or, better, to follow the Alport road to that village and trace the river upwards from there.

Youlgreave to Matlock. Far preferable to the main road through Rowsley is that over Stanton Moor, descending to Darley Dale. Turn sharp right over the river a mile below Alport. For Stanton village and the Moor (p. 126) turn up to the left half a mile farther. A somewhat hilly road runs right round the moor, and motorists can thus enjoy something of the scenery, but for the real joy of the Edge it is necessary to leave the car and walk over the top. Less than 1½ miles up the valley the road again forks: Robin Hood's Stride and the Cratcliffe Rocks lie to the right just beyond the fork; Rowtor Rocks are to the left, near Birchover.

For Matlock turn to the left in another 1½ miles and descend from Winster to Darley Dale.

Youlgreave to Arbor Low. Follow the Ashbourne road west from the village to the fork about three-quarters of a mile from the Church. In less than three-quarters of a mile farther branch to the right and then take the second turning on the left. This is known as the Long Rake and leads over the wide upland on which Arbor Low is situated. The path to the circle will be found on the left in about 2 miles. Motorists can turn in through the gateway on the main road, along the rough road leading to the ticket office and café. The stone circle is reached by following the path to the left of the café.

Arbor Low

is more than 1,200 feet above the sea, and apart from its archaeological associations is worth visiting on account of the wonderful view it commands over the uplands between the Dove and the Wye.

(**Admission** 6*d*., children half-price. **Open** from 9 a.m. to dusk. Sunday from 2 p.m.)

Arbor Low has always been considered the chief antiquarian feature of Derbyshire. It has been named " the Stonehenge of the Midlands," though it will not bear comparison with the immense stone circle of Salisbury Plain. It consists of a circle of rough unhewn stones, mostly from 6 to 8 feet long and 3 or 4 feet broad in the widest part, of variable thickness and extremely irregular in shape.

About thirty of these huge limestone blocks are to be seen, many lying on the ground in an oblique position. Smaller stones are irregularly scattered within the circle, and near the centre are three larger ones, conjectured to have formed part of a cromlech or altar. The circle is surrounded by a deep ditch, outside which is a mound, or vallum. The area encompassed by the ditch is about 50 yards in diameter, the width of the ditch is about 5 yards, and the height of the vallum, although probably much reduced by time, is still from 4 to 6 feet. The whole circumference is computed to be about 170 yards. There are two entrances, facing respectively north and south, each several yards in width. Many of the stones which originally formed this ancient structure have become buried

under the accumulations of hundreds of years and others are incorporated in neighbouring walls.

A barrow of extreme antiquity, on the eastern side of the southern entrance, was opened in 1845, a shoulder-blade and antler of a large red deer being found during the excavation. Beneath its highest part a flat stone was discovered, about 5 feet long by 3 feet wide, lying horizontally; on removing this a small six-sided cavity, formed by ten stones, and having a flooring of three similar stones neatly pointed, was exposed. Within this space were found a quantity of calcined human bones; there were also a rude kidney-shaped instrument made of flint, a pin made from the leg-bone of a small deer, and a piece of spherical iron pyrites.

Visitors who wonder at this choice of a village site may be reminded that: " In Neolithic times large areas of the British Isles were essentially lands of forest and marsh, and so uninhabitable by a people in a low state of culture. Such regions as the limestone hills of Derbyshire were in those times open spaces, and were soon inhabited. The people lived on the downs and moorlands in simple pastoral communities, herding their sheep, cattle and goats." (*The English Village*, H. Peake.)

The Long Rake goes on to meet a lane between Monyash (1¾ miles right—*see* p. 130) and the Ashbourne–Buxton road near Parsley Hay Station.

IV.—TO OVER HADDON AND THE LATHKIL VALLEY

This is a charming excursion through one of the best examples of glen scenery in Derbyshire.

For walkers, it is best to take bus or train to Bakewell (*see* p. 79). Motorists can drive as far as Over Haddon, but there is only a footpath through the Dale.

Leave Bakewell by the road ascending beside the church, avoiding the left turn near the top of the hill. Keep straight over the crossroads half a mile from Bakewell, and at the next choice turn left. The road climbs the hillside, and with each yard the view increases in extent and interest. On reaching **Over Haddon** village, turn first to the left for the sake of the splendid view over the Lathkil which unexpectedly opens up, then turn right to go through the village; the road route down to the Dale begins at the other end of the village street, where we bear down to the left past the church (*cars must not be parked at the foot of the hill, and are best left at the top*). The road ends at a mill, but the path continues along the northern side of the stream—becoming increasingly beautiful. **Lathkil Dale** gains its impressiveness more from its narrowness and the abrupt slope of its flanking hills than from any particular size or grandeur of detail. From the point where the glen opens out again, a rough track runs up the Over Haddon–Monyash road and it is possible to return that way, but it is worth while keeping in the Dale, taking the right-hand branch—**Ricklow Dale**—where it forks. The source of the river (in a cave) is passed in half a mile and the road is reached at a point about a mile from Monyash and 3 from Over Haddon.

Monyash

Monyash is 5 miles from Bakewell by the high-road and about $1\frac{1}{4}$ miles from the Ashbourne to Buxton highway (at the Hurdlow Station turning). Buses run to Bakewell and Buxton.

Monyash **Church** (St. Leonard's) is a twelfth-century building. In the chancel are three sedilia and a piscina beneath a Norman arcade, and the church also has a very old chest.

In the village is an ancient market cross. Of interest, and reached from the top of Lathkil Dale, is **One Ash Grange,**

which was one of the " granges " or houses from which the monks of Roche Abbey administered their land holdings. The Grange was for long tenanted by a Quaker family with whom John Bright was connected. One Ash was the name he gave to his Rochdale residence. It was in Lathkil Dale, too, that he met his future wife.

Over Haddon to Alport. From the mill below Over Haddon the river-side path continues downstream and provides a lovely walk as far as Alport (*see* p. 127), whence one may pick up a bus for the return to Bakewell.

V.—TO WIRKSWORTH AND BRASSINGTON ROCKS

Wirksworth lies about 2 miles south of Cromford by a road that is best traversed by car or bus on account of the mile-long climb past the Black Rocks.

Wirksworth

an old market town, centre of a one-time busy lead-mining industry, is interesting as the scene of some of the incidents in George Eliot's *Adam Bede*. The workshop of Adam and the home of Dinah Bede are still pointed out.

The old pulpit from which Elizabeth Evans preached is in the Bede Memorial Methodist Church while various relics may be seen on application to the Methodist minister.

The **Parish Church** (St. Mary's) is a thirteenth-century Early English structure, restored by Sir Gilbert Scott. Remains of the Norman church which preceded it, and of an earlier Saxon edifice, were carefully pieced into the restored building. Among these remains is one, of Saxon origin, in the north aisle, representing the chief events in the life of Christ. The church is held by some to have originated in a chapelry dedicated to St. Helena in the days of the Roman occupation. The north chancel aisle contains the fine Renaissance tomb of Anthony Gell, who founded the Grammar School in 1576. In the north transept is a stained window designed by Burne-Jones and a fine old Norman font. The church roof was entirely reconstructed and lowered in 1926, this exposing much more of the fine tower. To the north-west of the church is a fine preaching cross—probably Saxon.

Wirksworth is completely honeycombed by old lead mines, many of them of Roman origin. In the Moot Hall, Chapel Lane, are held twice a year the *Great Barmote Courts* for the Soke and Wapentake of Wirksworth, and here is deposited an ancient copper dish used as a standard for measuring ore. Some of the lead mines appear to have been worked at the beginning of the second century A.D. In 1952, to commemorate the centenary of the passing of the Mineral Courts Act, a pure lead medallion, mined and smelted locally, was sent to Queen Elizabeth. The " **Well-Dressings,**" which take place in Whit-week, attract large crowds both from the surrounding parishes and farther afield (*see* also Tissington Well-Dressings —p. 149). The district including Wirksworth and surrounding parishes was at one time known as the " King's Field " and from it the Sovereign through the Duchy of Lancaster was entitled to a proportion of all lead ore mined.

There are several alternative routes by which to return to Matlock. One of the best is to fork left at the north end of the town to reach Middleton and then descend by the Via Gellia and so to Cromford.

Harborough Rocks, Brassington and Rainster Rocks. The Wirksworth trip may be extended to include these two sets of rocks, which, though less fantastic than the extraordinary collection over by Birchover and Stanton Moor, provide a very interesting excursion. From Wirksworth the direction is westward from the parish church by the Ashbourne road and a lane diverging right from this in a quarter of a mile. To the right of the road, 3 miles from Wirksworth, are **Harborough Rocks,** an outcrop of magnesium limestone surmounting a plateau over a 1,000 feet high and affording a fine view from the summit. There is a cave and on top of the rocks some interesting shapes including *The Pulpit, The Font* and *The Chair.*

Farther along the road is the village of **Brassington,** where St. James's Church possesses some Norman work in the tower, porch and south aisle. The pillars of the north aisle are of Ashford marble and were added at a restoration in 1881.

Just under a mile north-west of the village are the **Brassington,** or **Rainster Rocks.** These may be approached by a footpath leading over the hill behind the church. A broken mass of limestone boulders rising from the valley, with ivy and fir trees, these rocks are a favourite haunt of climbers.

From Brassington one may go northward to Longcliffe, then turn right for **Grange Mill,** at the head of the Via Gellia, and return thence to Cromford and Matlock.

VI.—TO ALTON TOWERS

Alton is a very popular rallying-place of Midland folk, and to which many coach excursions run from all parts. It certainly provides an interesting trip from Matlock.

Alton lies some 8 miles south-west of Ashbourne, in the most beautiful part of the Churnet Valley. The village stands on the slope of a sandstone hill that presents a bold scarp to the valley below. On the summit, rising flush with the precipice, is **Alton Castle,** once garrisoned for Cromwell. Many visitors make the mistake of leaving the village unvisited, but it well repays the climb from the station. Among other features note the solid cylindrical "lock-up."

The feature which brings so many people to Alton, however, is the estate known as—

Alton Towers

(**Open** daily, admission charge; free car park. Facilities include restaurant and refreshment kiosks, aerial cable cars, amusement park, boating, scenic and model railways, pony rides and paddling pool.)

with its beautiful gardens. In recent years these have become a very popular resort, band concerts being given. There is a large restaurant in the grounds.

The entrance gateway to the grounds of the Towers is close to the station, on the side opposite the village. The drive makes a circuit, but a wide walk starts from the lodge to the right and ascends through the woods, with several  short flights of steps, to a large gravel plot at the back of the mansion, whence we pass between walls and under an archway to the terrace that overlooks the gardens, and commands a full view of the mansion.

The external appearance of Alton Towers is very imposing. The sky-line is diversified with towers, pinnacles and battlements, and the main body of the building, though it follows no regular plan, presents a combination of solidity and lightness which is seldom equalled in our more modern mansions. It was begun in 1814, by the fifteenth Earl of Shrewsbury, and completed by his son, to a great extent from the designs and under the superintendence of Pugin. The mansion is now a ruin, but forms an imposing background to the gardens.

On the right side of the broad terrace-walk on which we now stand are the **Gardens,** occupying a lovely dell which descends to the valley of the Churnet. They are a maze of walks, terraces, arbours, steps, rocks, flower-beds and other attractions—mostly artificial—which as a whole justify the inscription running round an open Corinthian Temple, a copy of the Temple of Lysicates at Athens, just below the bridge that spans one entrance to the gardens. "He made the desert smile." This reference is to the sixteenth Earl of Shrewsbury, whose bust is within the Temple. A feature of the scene is the abundance of evergreen trees and shrubs—cedar, araucarias, and other conifers in great variety—while in the late spring the rhododendron blooms on every side.

Crossing the bridge, we pass a lake walled off by a parapet on the left, and several walks into the Gardens on the right. On the left of the second of these walks is a group of sandstone rocks strangely piled one upon another. A furlong or so along the *Earl's Drive* is the *Gothic Temple,* a favourite viewpoint, from which the Towers are well seen over the Gardens.

Alton to **Ellastone,** 5 miles. From the Towers keep along the terrace-walk and pass the stables—a quadrangular block—on the left. A footpath leads straight on across a field or two into a lane, turning right along which we soon drop into a pretty valley and, passing on the right a remarkable group of eight yews, on a mound, ascend to **Wootton Lodge,** a tall Elizabethan mansion of stone and glass, incorporating parts of the earlier medieval house, which has been described as one of the most beautiful and romantic houses in England. The Lodge, built on an outcrop of rock and partly surrounded by water, lies in densely wooded country in the shadow of the Weaver Hills and is almost certainly the work of the mason-architect Robert Smithson who came from Nottingham in 1580 and was responsible for Hardwick Hall in Derbyshire. During the Civil War it was a Royalist stronghold, and in 1643 was besieged and captured by Oliver Cromwell who burnt down the outer fortifications on the entrance front. It is probably the original of Donnithorne Chase in George Eliot's *Adam Bede.* It is now the home of Major Alan Rook, the well-known poet of the Hitler war. From the Lodge a corner may be cut off by a path ("private") which joins the road again at the main entrance-gate to the drive, a mile short of **Ellastone.** From Ellastone (*see* p. 155) to Ashbourne the distance by high road (bus route) is 5 miles.

VII.—TO CHESTERFIELD

Banks. — *Barclays,* Knifesmith Gate; *Lloyds, Midland* and *Westminster,* all in Market Place; *National Provincial,* New Square; *Williams Deacon's,* Stephenson Place; *Yorkshire Penny,* Central Pavement.

Civic Theatre, cinemas, etc.
Early Closing Day.—Wednesday.
Information Bureau.—At the Public Library, Corporation Street.
Population.—68,230.
Post Office.—High Street.

Only some 10 miles north-east of Matlock by a road traversing the breezy heights between the Derwent and the Amber is Chesterfield, interesting not only on account of the famous crooked spire of its parish church, but as a busy and progressive town with a good market and a number of modern shops.

The Crooked Spire has been the subject of much conjecture, but there seems little reason to doubt that the cause of the malformation was the use of unseasoned timber in its construction.

The **Church,** famous for its Crooked Spire, which dates from 1400, and leans some 10 feet out of the straight (height 228 feet), bears the unusual dedication of Our Lady and All Saints. It dates from the thirteenth and fourteenth centuries, and will well repay a visit. The font is Saxon, and the magnificent Parclose Screen across the south transept was erected c. 1500. It is the only parish church in the country which has a Corona of five chapels (all beautifully furnished) behind the great central altar, which stands under the tower. There are altar tombs and massive wall monuments to five generations of the Foljambe (Earl of Liverpool's) family, in a state of perfect preservation, dating from 1510 to 1598. Two magnificent candelabra, with elaborate wrought-iron pendants, presented by a merchant adventurer in 1760, adorn the Lady Chapel and St. Catherine's Chapel. It is thought that they are treasure trove from some Spanish ship, intended originally for some great church in South America. There is a medieval processional cross, for centuries in the hands of the Hunloke family, restored to the parish church some 40 years ago. Much of the excellent stained glass is by Christopher Webb and Sir Ninian Comper. A disastrous fire in 1961 caused considerable damage in the Church, but this has now been repaired.

Prominent men associated with Chesterfield include Charles Darwin, the naturalist, who was educated at the Grammar School, and George Stephenson, the father of railways, who spent his declining years here and is buried in Trinity Church. The Stephenson Memorial Hall houses the public library and the Civic Theatre.

At Old Whittington, about 2 miles north of the town centre, is **"Revolution House,"** a little stone building with a thatched roof, once an inn which in 1688 sheltered William Cavendish, fourth Earl of Devonshire, and a few friends who, incensed with the policy of James II, met to arrange to bring William of Orange to the throne. The house was acquired by the Chesterfield Corporation in 1938, restored and furnished with seventeenth-century furniture. The House is open to the public from Easter to end of September, daily except Wednesdays, from 11 a.m. (*free*). The Whittington buses from the centre of the town stop at Revolution House.

The return to Matlock may be varied by going westward from Chesterfield to Baslow, by a fine though hilly road over the moors, and thence southward through Chatsworth Park; or one can retrace the Matlock road as far as the *Red Lion Inn*, nearly 5 miles from Chesterfield, where the right-hand road is taken at the fork, and so down to Rowsley.

VIII.—TO DERBY

Airport.—Castle Donington, 8 miles.
Banks.—*Barclays*, St. James' Street; *Lloyds*, Irongate; *Martins* and *National Provincial*, Market Place; *Midland*, St. Peter's Street; *Westminster*, Corn Market and Irongate; *Williams Deacon's*, Corn Market; *Derby Savings Bank*, Friar Gate; *C.W.S.*, Wardwick; *District*, St. Peter's Street.

Distances by Road.—London, 128 miles; Sheffield, 36; Matlock 16; Buxton (*via* Ashbourne), 33.
Early Closing Day.—Wednesday.
Hotels.—*See* p. 10.
Population.—About 132,000.
Post Office.—Victoria Street.

This ancient town, the old-world aspect of which has now almost disappeared, is the seat of a number of important industries, best known among which is the world-famous Rolls-Royce Company. There are a number of good shops in the town, which is generally at its busiest on Fridays—market day. Motorists coming from the south and making for the Peak District are served by a very useful by-pass which makes a wide sweep round the western side of the town.

Derby's chief architectural possession is the **Cathedral Church of All Saints,** a Parish Church raised to Cathedral status in 1927. In 1723 the previous medieval church, in ruinous condition, was demolished except for the tower. To this, James Gibb, a pupil of Wren, was commissioned to add a new building in Renaissance style. In its simplicity and proportions it is one of the finest of its type in the country. It possesses a remarkable wrought iron Chancel screen and other works by Robert Bakewell. There are some interesting monuments including the tomb of the Countess of Shrewsbury (Bess of Hardwick) and a fine collection of old and modern plate. In 1964 restoration work was begun by Sebastian Comper and included two large stained glass windows designed by Ceri Richards.

Of interest to archaeologists especially is the old **Bridge Chapel of St. Mary,** in Bridge Gate. The original Chapel was a small square building on a buttress of the bridge; in course of time it was extended, and in the eighteenth century a new bridge was built, on a different alignment from the old. After passing through a variety of experiences the Chapel has been well restored; occasional services are held.

Of more general interest is the **Royal Crown Derby China Factory,** which may be visited by arrangement during working hours. The factory is in Osmaston Road, which continues south from St. Peter's Street, and near the Arboretum. Crown Derby China has held an unrivalled position in the ceramic world since the manufacture of porcelain was begun in the town in 1750. The productions surpass in purity of " body," richness of design, and opulence of colour the most famous pieces of the artist-workmen employed by the Duesburys of the seventeenth century.

Near the Post Office, in Victoria Street, is the **Central Library and Museum,** comprising a lending and reference library, including collections of Derbyshire literature and prints and drawings of unrivalled local interest to the antiquary. The Museum contains a good selection of relics of the old-time Derbyshire mines and a unique working model of old Midlands Railway stock. The iron gates by the side of the Museum should be noticed, having been transplanted bodily from the old Derwent Silk Mill. In the Strand, behind the Library, and similar in its architecture, is the **Corporation Art Gallery,** which contains a fine permanent collection of pictures by Wright of Derby as well as providing for the display of visiting collections. A considerable addition in modern style and fronting to the Strand and Cheapside has recently been made to the Library, Museum and Art Gallery, which has enabled very considerable increases to be made in the facilities available to visitors.

Much redevelopment is taking place in the town centre in order to meet ever growing traffic densities and changing shopping habits and much more is planned. The Main Centre, shopping and offices precinct, between London Road and Traffic Street is an example.

To Wolfscote Dale & Hartington
To Buxton
Alstonefield
Lode Mill
Alsop-en-le Dale
Shining Tor
R. DOVE
L.M. & R.
Hopedale
Pack Horse Bridge
Mill Dale
To Wetton
MILL DALE
Stepping Stones
Farm
New Inns Hotel
Stepping Stones
Weir
Bailey Hill
1010 FT
1136 FT
Stepping Stones
Ravens Tor
Hanson Grange
HALL DALE
Weir
Spring
The Nab
HURTS
NABS
DALE
Foot Bridge
Dove Holes
1085 FT
WOOD
Stepping Stones
Weir
Pickering Cave
Ilam Rock
Pickering Tor
Natural Arch
Lion's Head Rock
DOVEDALE
Stepping Stones
1103 FT
Reynard's Cave
ILAM TOPS
Weir
Natural Arch
Air Cottage
Weir
SHARPLOW DALE
Farm
To Tissington
Tissington Spires
Jacob's Ladder
Weir
Moor Barn
Weir
Lovers' Leap
Twelve Apostles
Waterfalls
Waterfalls
Dovedale Castle
Rocks
Waterfall
1000
BUNSTER HILL
Stepping Stones
R. DOVE
THORPE CLOUD
To Manifold Valley
Izaak Walton Hotel
CAR PARK
Foot Bridge
942 FT
PARK
Ilam
Ilam Hall
Chu.
Weir
Reveril Hotel
Thorpe Cloud Sta.
R. Manifold
Thorpe Mill
Thorpe Cloud
To Ashbourne
To Tissington
To Tissington & Ashbourne
0   ¼   ½ MILE
Main Road
Other Roads
Footpaths

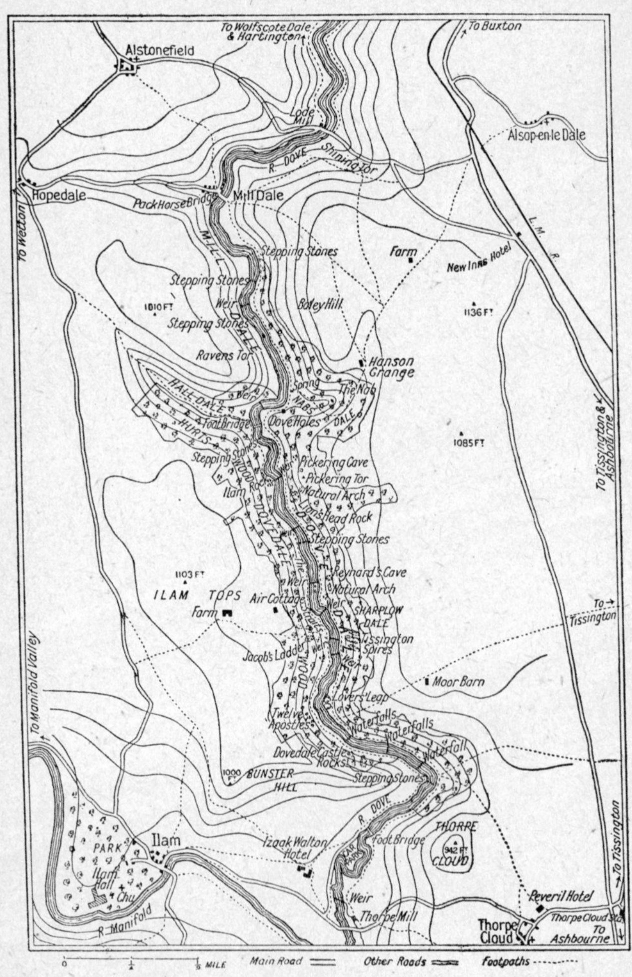

DOVEDALE

DOVEDALE

Access.—Dovedale runs more or less parallel with the Ashbourne-Buxton main road which is some 8 miles west of the Matlock-Bakewell road and railway. Buses connect Matlock and Ashbourne and also run between Ashbourne and Thorpe and Ilam.

Motorists wishing to walk through the Dale and return to their cars may be reminded that there are parking facilities at the hotels. There is a parking place at the south end of the Dale, reached by the lane diverging to the right from the drive to the *Izaak Walton Hotel*, but it is inadvisable to depend upon finding a vacant piece of ground at Milldale.

Dovedale proper extends northwards from Thorpe Cloud to Dove Holes, a distance of not more than 2 miles. The path leads up the Derbyshire side, and those who make the *Izaak Walton*, on the Staffordshire bank, their starting-place must cross either the foot-bridge, a little north of the hotel, or the stepping stones still higher up, at the first bend of the river : those with no taste for the latter should bear this in mind before passing the bridge. From Thorpe the shortest way is by path down the deepening glade to the right of Thorpe Cloud.

Those who wish to see as much as possible within the limits of a comfortable day's excursion are recommended to drive to Thorpe, *viâ* Tissington, then to walk through Dovedale to Mill Dale, and on to Wetton and Thor's Cave, returning direct from Wetton to Thorpe through Ilam, a round of about 12 miles. Whatever else is omitted the walk through Dovedale from Thorpe to Mill Dale must certainly be included. A gem that is too often omitted is Beresford Dale, a comfortable walk from Hartington and actually accessible by car by turning left before reaching Hulme End and left again in about a mile. The lane down is rough, but safe.

MATLOCK TO DOVEDALE OR ASHBOURNE

The road route runs *viâ* Cromford and thence up the Via Gellia to Grange Mill, where turn left for Tissington and Dovedale (Thorpe): 14 miles.

The principal features are described in connection with the walking route, and the only special note necessary relates to the *Ford* by which one leaves the Ashbourne road and crosses to Tissington. Except after very heavy rain, this is passable by most cars; in case of doubt, follow the road for another $3\frac{1}{2}$ miles towards Ashbourne, and then turn sharp back to right along the Buxton road for $1\frac{1}{2}$ miles to the gates of the Tissington estate (*see* p. 149). This route passes through **Fenny Bentley**, with a picturesque remnant of the Old Hall of the Beresfords. St. Edmund's Church contains the tomb of Thomas Beresford (*d.* 1473) and his wife. Thomas fought at Agincourt and much of the house he built still stands (farmhouse opposite church). The tomb, a century later in design, bears their shrouded effigies and also depicts their sixteen sons and five daughters.

Walkers can choose from several routes between Matlock and Dovedale. The best are through Parwich, whence they may proceed westward by road and footpath to Lode Mill, which is about $1\frac{1}{2}$ miles above the beginning of Dovedale proper at Dove Holes, or they may follow a path southward to Tissington and a lane thence alongside the exterior of the *Peveril of the Peak Hotel*'s north-eastern boundary, at Thorpe, or from Tissington enter the dale in its central part under Tissington Spires.

From Matlock the way to Parwich begins with the **Via Gellia,** which is followed to Grange Mill, some 5 miles from Matlock Bath. Here the Ashbourne road goes off on the left, in about 2 miles arriving at Longcliffe. About $1\frac{1}{2}$ miles past Longcliffe, and opposite a lane which comes down on the left from Brassington, a footpath strikes up on the right across the south end of White Edge to the tiny village of **Ballidon,** whence another path, starting about a quarter of a mile up the lane to the right, leads up into another lane at right angles which goes down a pretty valley, at the foot of which is **Parwich** (*Sycamore Inn,* close by Church).

Hence (*a*) for **Lode Mill** (*Mill Dale*) proceed by road to the large farm of *Parwich Leas* (1 mile), a little beyond which a path strikes up on the left and, leaving the church and farms of Alsop-en-le-Dale below on the right, ascends diagonally into (2 miles) the Ashbourne–Buxton road, which it enters about 100 yards to the left of a road that strikes off opposite the *New Inn* and drops by a very steep pitch to **Lode Mill** (3 miles). Hence the road out of the valley rises again to **Alstonfield** (4 miles); for **Wetton** and **Thor's Cave** (p. 148). A second road follows the river-side to **Milldale** (3½ miles). The path from Milldale down **Dovedale** to Ilam and Thorpe is described in the reverse direction on pp. 142–4.

(*b*) A footpath, succeeded by a lane, leads from Parwich to **Tissington** (2 miles; p. 149), whence an avenue leads to the Ashbourne–Buxton road (2½ miles), after crossing which proceed by a lane which comes out opposite the *Dog and Partridge Hotel*. The road to Thorpe and the foot of Dovedale starts on the right-hand side of the hotel.

The Dale

Attractive Dovedale is a narrow gorge-like valley, some three miles in length, with wooded slopes rising almost sheer from the crystal stream. Here and there the walls of foliage are broken by limestone rocks that mimic every variety of architectural shape. Bastion, basilica and buttress, minaret and pinnacle, pyramid and arch, turret and spire, tower and cupola, follow one another in bewildering fascination.

It has been said, possibly without exaggeration, that the visitor may come straight from Switzerland or the Pyrenees, and " be ready to acknowledge that Europe does not yield another picture so sweet in sylvan beauty, or so changeful in its fairy-like combination of wood and rock and water " as this most lovely part of the valley of the Dove.

The valleys of Cumberland and Wales, of the Yorkshire Pennines and the High Peak District have an unlikeness to the peculiar charm of the Dove. They are wide-spreading and profuse in their beauty, while Dovedale is a scene of hemmed-in loveliness, of compressed beauty. In this very minuteness is its charm. It is a glen diversified with clefts and dingles, alternate juts and recesses of rocks, wooded hollows and towering heights, and its flower-decked banks are washed by the foam-crisped wavelets of the wilful stream.

The modern Izaak Walton will have reason to pause time after time as he wanders along the banks of the Dove. Here he may see a grayling, there a trout, each with its nose directed against the stream, waiting for the food, natural or artificial, that the stream carries towards it. For the information of the fly-fisher who wishes to follow the example set by the author of *The Compleat Angler*, it may be recorded here that fishing may be had by guests at certain hotels in the vicinity (*see* pp. 16–17). The stream is so clear that it seems to cast a light upwards through the shady recesses of the overhanging cliffs. Along the gorge the Dove wanders over its limestone bed, now gurgling against the rocks, now circling in eddies, now splashing in little waterfalls, now calmly resting in pools, amidst which wait the trout and the grayling for their " daily bread." The stream is broken by a succession of little weirs— partly artificial and holding back the water in a manner which will only be appreciated by the angler. Around are hawthorn, hazel and a multitude of other trees, shrubs, and wild flowers.

In springtime, when every little knoll is carpeted with primroses, or in the late autumn, when the foliage assumes its ruddiest tint, the dale wears its loveliest aspect. The preponderance of ash in its more thickly wooded parts defers till very late in the summer the period at which winter utterly strips it of its leafy honours, and even then its undergrowth of bracken and the sombre yews which take roots in the crevices of its steepest crags maintain a contrast of colour till the vivid green of the sprouting larch ushers in returning vegetation.

THROUGH DOVEDALE

The shortest approach to Dovedale from Thorpe is by a lane alongside the exterior of the *Peveril of the Peak Hotel*'s north-eastern boundary and the footpath thence leading to the right of the distinctive cone* of **Thorpe Cloud** (942 feet) and dropping down the tiny Lin Dale to the Stepping Stones (*see* below).

A better route, however, turns to the right at the beginning of Thorpe Village and, after crossing the side of Thorpe Cloud, descends to the bridge over the Dove near Thorpe Mill. Cross the river, here giving no indication of its beauty a little higher up, and branch to the right from the drive to the *Isaak Walton Hotel*. In 500 yards the car-park is passed, and a little farther a footbridge is reached. A path continues on either side of the Dove, which forces its way out of its narrow

* The hill, or cone, is actually a ridge and looks quite different from the other side.

ravine between **Bunster Hill** (1,000 feet) and Thorpe Cloud, as far as the Stepping Stones, where the shorter route is joined.

At this point the river takes an abrupt turn and the narrow part of the Dale commences. The track ascends on the Derbyshire bank, i.e. the left bank (or right-hand side proceeding upstream), all the way. After crossing a rich greensward it climbs to one of the best viewpoints in the Dale—Sharplow Point.

On the Staffordshire side, as we approach Sharplow Point, the woods climb from the water's edge to the brow of the hills, but they are broken by a series of steep and rugged limestone crags which have been fancifully named the *Twelve Apostles*. **Sharplow Point** (also known as the " Lover's Leap ") itself is a bare face of rock a few yards to the left of the path. Occupying a sharp angle of the stream, and standing high above it, it commands a beautiful vista in both directions. Northwards the dale is seen becoming narrower and narrower till there is only room for the river to pass between the perpendicular cliffs which hem it in. Southwards the cone of Thorpe Cloud rises most effectively, and secures that entire exclusion of extraneous objects which is a characteristic of Dovedale views. Eastward a grassy glade, by which Tissington may be reached in about 2 miles, ascends steeply to the right of **Tissington Spires,** as a group of jagged and lofty rock-pinnacles is called. They somewhat resemble the famous needle rocks of Cheddar, and though in reality they are only scarped projections of the high ground beneath them, they have every appearance from below of being virgin peaks. They are best seen from a little way farther on our route.

Beyond Sharplow Point the track again descends to the water's edge, passing, on the Staffordshire side, a deeply fissured mass of rock, to which the name *Dovedale Church* has been given. A little farther, we have on the right, high above us, **Reynard's Cave,** a wide-portalled alcove. In front of the cave is a large natural arch perforating a ridge of rock only a few feet wide. It is worth visiting for the sake of the lovely views of the Straits of Dovedale, as the narrowest part of the glen is called.

We now approach the narrowest part of the dale, appropriately called the **Straits.** At this point the Staffordshire side is quite impassable, and the Derbyshire side offers the alternative of a narrow causeway, often flooded, and a better route at higher land. The beauty of the glen hereabouts is of a very high order; foliage and water are brought into their closest contrast. Hawthorn, hazel and wilding creepers encroach on the track, and darkling yews grow out of the chinks in the perpendicular crags. A rock in front, on the Derbyshire side, is, with a fair show of reason, called the **Lion's Head** (best seen from the north side).

A few strides farther, and we have left the main part of Dovedale behind us. It ends as it began—thoroughly unique. Nature has even given it a gateway, the posts whereof are two towering crags: **Ilam Rock,** a leaning pinnacle, on the left, and **Pickering Tor** to the right. Looking back between these rugged portals, after we have passed through them, we find another remarkable view of the dale, scarcely inferior in beauty to any of those already described.

Everyone who has enjoyed the beauty of Dovedale will be gratified to learn that nearly 1,000 acres of it, including **Hurt's Wood,** above Ilam Rock, on the Staffordshire side, is in the careful hands of the National Trust, while protective covenants are held by them over a further 900 acres.

Those who have no wish to continue to Mill Dale can cross the second foot-bridge beyond Ilam Rock and make their way up through Hall Dale to the Ilam–Wetton road. Others, passing over a pleasant meadow, again come to a rocky path and suddenly encounter three huge-mouthed caverns called **Dove Holes.** These caves mark the junction of Dovedale and Mill Dale: on the right **Nabs Dale** offers a way up to Hanson Grange and the main road near Alsop-en-le-Dale.

The main route, however, passes into—

Mill Dale

which suffers, unfortunately, by comparison with Dovedale. Steep hills rise from the stream on both sides, but they are only scantily varied with rock, and there is very little relief of foliage.

The scenery soon begins to recover, however. If Mill Dale cannot vie with Dovedale it is nevertheless a very charming little valley on its own account, especially that part just below the tiny hamlet of **Milldale,** where *refreshments* can be obtained. (The road to the left through the hamlet climbs up through Hopedale to **Wetton.**) At the southern end of the hamlet is a pack-horse bridge now scheduled as a National Monument. Half a mile above the bridge by the road on the left bank is **Lode Mill** (*refreshments*), whence the road goes up (right) to the *New Inns Hotel* and (left) to **Alstonfield** (p. 54). A path continues on the right bank (upstream) of the river, more National Trust ground, and in about a mile enters **Wolfscote Dale,** another lovely reach, enclosed partly by wooded crags, partly by steep grass slopes.

At the end of it an open strath is reached, and the path crosses to a foot-bridge giving access to the Staffordshire bank. Over this bridge turn to the right to enter—

Beresford Dale

This is one of the prettiest parts of the Dove. Steep limestone crags, finely overgrown with beech and other trees, enclose it on both sides, while the pleasant greensward between the river and the rocks makes it on a warm summer's day quite a little Paradise. The Dale is less than a mile long, but it presents an epitome of the beauties of the whole of Dovedale. It forms the theme of that " Second Part " which Cotton added to Walton's *Compleat Angler.* Walton tells us that the Dale is not far " from Mr. Cotton's house, below which place this delicate river takes a swift career betwixt many mighty rocks, much higher and bigger than St. Paul's Church (old St. Paul's Cathedral) before it was burnt." The rocks mentioned by Walton are well wooded, and many are pierced by caves. Before recrossing to the Derbyshire side the path passes a sharp pointed rock rising like a stake from the river; this part of which has in consequence been named *Pike Pool* —described by the " Viator " of Waltonian days as " the oddest sight I ever saw."

On private ground, on the Staffordshire side of the stream, are the Prospect Tower and Cotton's Cave. The former is a modern structure standing on the site of the original tower, which it was made to resemble as much as was possible through the guidance of old drawings. The tower was in the grounds of Beresford Hall, Charles Cotton's residence. In front of its entrance is the old bowling-green.

Cotton's Cave was one of the hiding-places to which Charles Cotton was accustomed to flee when hard-pressed by duns. That it was well suited for the purpose is indicated by the fact that its mouth is so hidden by brushwood and vegetation that it is very difficult to find. Within is a flat, dry shelf of rock whereon Cotton was wont to spread his pallet and where he lay in hiding till the search for him had ceased and the thwarted bailiffs had left the neighbourhood.

Everyone knows Izaak Walton, the Prince of Anglers, but **Charles Cotton** is a less familiar personage. He was born at Beresford Hall, which had been inherited by his mother. He received a fair education and made various contributions to literature. On the death of his father he entered into possession of an estate which had been impoverished by extravagance and lawsuits. To discharge his own and his father's debts he disposed of a part of the property, but, being naturally extravagant, fresh debts accrued and to avoid his creditors or their agents he again and again sought refuge in the caves of the neighbourhood. His second wife had a jointure of £1,500 a year, but even that did not free him from money troubles. Finally, he was obliged to leave Beresford Hall, never to return. He is said to have died in a garret in London at the age of 57.

The Hall was purchased in 1825 by Field-Marshal Viscount Beresford, who bequeathed it to his kinsman, Beresford Hope. At the time of the testator's death, it had become ruinous, and was pulled down a few years later.

At the northern end of Beresford Dale, scarcely to be seen among the trees on the Staffordshire side, is the famous **Fishing House,**

erected by Charles Cotton in 1674. It is a small stone structure of one room only, built with the grey limestone of the district with roof high-pitched and surmounted by a stone pillar and a ball. The legend " Piscatoribus sacrum, 1674," with Cotton's and Walton's intertwined initials beneath it, may still be seen over the circular-headed door by visitors privileged to view the place; but the full-dress portraits of the two friends, with which the interior was graced, have long disappeared, though the fireplace, the marble table and the old oak chairs remain.

A strange friendship was that of Izaak Walton and Charles Cotton. The one was the biographer of Donne, Wotton, Hooker, Herbert, and Sanderson; the other wrote the indecencies of *Virgile Travestie*; the one was the most pious of saints; the other the most profligate of sinners. Their companionship can only be accounted for by the attraction of opposites. The spirits of Izaak Walton and Charles Cotton haunt Dovedale. Dante is not more closely associated in history with Florence, nor Shakespeare with Stratford, than the Fleet Street draper and the young Derbyshire squire are with the banks of the Dove.

The path leaves the Dale, crosses a walled lane and bears to the right to reach—

Hartington

a picturesque village which gives the courtesy title of Marquis to the eldest sons of the Dukes of Devonshire. It is partly grouped round a large square. The position of the village with respect to some of the best Derbyshire scenery makes it a good centre for tourists, and for many walkers and cyclists there is the added attraction that the fine **Hartington Hall,** originally erected in 1350 and rebuilt in 1611, is now a Youth Hostel.

The Hall, in the right branch of the lane crossing the east end of the village, was built in 1611 by Hugh Bateman. It contains some fine carved oak and panelling and is a very good example of an early seventeenth-century house.

A thriving industry here is the manufacture of Stilton cheese.

The left branch of the lane leads to the **Church.** Dedicated to St. Giles and restored in 1858, it contains good Early English and Decorated work. The building is cruciform, and has a square western tower of the fourteenth century, probably unequalled in Derbyshire. The three bells date from 1636, 1637 and 1697 respectively. The windows of the church are unique for they represent a picture of the whole range of window development over a period of three centuries. There are a number of quaint gargoyles.

The best point from which to view the interior of the church is at the entrance to the most northerly pew. The old font, at the west end, is ornamented with window tracery which possibly represents certain of the original windows of the church.

The Manifold Valley

The Manifold, so called, it is said, from the many folds or turns it makes, is an important tributary of the Dove. Like the main stream, it rises in the neighbourhood of Axe Edge. Its entire course is beautiful; some who know both the Dove and the Manifold contend that parts of the Manifold Valley are superior in point of scenery to the more popular Dovedale. "It is more pastoral and less rugged," as well as more expansive than the other dales between Buxton and Ashbourne.

The beauties of the Manifold Valley are less easily accessible since the closing of the Manifold Light Railway, but buses bring it sufficiently near to enable half-day excursions to be made without undue hurry. From Thor's Cave downstream —the finest part of the valley—the only practicable walking route in many places is along the public footpath that has now supplanted the former railway line.

The best-known part of the valley is that immediately west of the village of Wetton (*see* p. 145), for here is **Thor's Cave,** a remarkable hollow in Wetton Low, a prominent eminence overlooking the Manifold. The floor of the cave is about 250 feet above the bed of the river. The opening, about 23 feet wide and 30 feet high, commands a fine view of the district. In the cave have been found arrowheads, bone combs and pins, iron adzes, bronze armillae, spindle wheels and rings and other personal ornaments, which were placed in the Derby museum. Human remains have also been found. The relics indicate that the cave was occupied by Celts, Romans and Anglo-Saxons.

By reason of its regularity, the arch at the entrance, as seen from the road, might readily be mistaken for a misplaced piece of masonry. The cave is effectively lighted to a considerable depth by a second opening on the right, almost as lofty as the principal one, but much narrower. Almost opposite this is a massive column, supporting arches which extend further inward. The effect of the light and of the size and proportion of the arches on returning to the entrance is very fine.

From Wetton Mill a good motor road now runs north along the line of the old railway track to Hulme End.

The principal feature of the valley, however, lies between Thor's Cave and Wetton Mill—the " swallows " through which, in dry weather, the river disappears for about 4 miles, to re-appear in the grounds of Ilam Hall (p. 149). The " swallows " are quite close to the road as it crosses the river at the foot of Redhurst Crag.

Rather less than a mile below Thor's Cave is **Beeston Tor,** a huge mass of limestone rising 200 feet from the river. At the foot of the rock is **St. Bertram's Cave.** The aperture is so narrow that, if the saint used the cave, he must have been extremely spare in build. Animal remains, pottery, rings, fibulas, etc., have been found in the cave.

By crossing the river-bed at this point and following the footpath that goes up a steep ascent for about half a mile, a fine view is obtained. The prospect embraces the remains of

Throwley Old Hall, a short distance away on the opposite side of the hill.

The history of the place begins with Oliver de Meverell, in the reign of King John, but the building, now in ruins, dates only from 1603. Even in its present condition it is easy to see that it once fully merited Erdeswick's description as " a fair ancient house and goodly demesne, being the seat of the Meverells, a very ancient house of gentlemen and of goodly living, equalling the best sort of gentleman in the shire."
The last of the Meverells was the wife of the fourth Baron Cromwell, created, 1625, Viscount Lecade and Earl of Ardglass. The second earl's widow became Charles Cotton's second wife.

When the water is plentiful, the Hamps unites with the river Manifold near Beeston Tor, but during dry weather the stream disappears through openings in the limestone rocks in its beds, a little higher up its course. To this disappearance the village of **Waterfall,** on a feeder of the Hamps, owes its name.
The Manifold reappears in the very beautiful grounds of the Hall at—

Ilam

a trim model village. The Hall, which, with the grounds, belongs to the National Trust, is pseudo-Gothic in character, though erected during the last century. It has a claim to antiquity, however, for in the grounds of the ancient well of St. Bertram, an Anglo-Saxon hermit. It is now one of the most delightfully situated of the Derbyshire Youth Hostels. The road to the left, at the entrance gate, leads to the **Church,** which has a curiously-carved Norman font and a blocked-up Saxon doorway. South of the chancel is St. Bertram's Chapel, with the saint's tomb; north of it is a beautiful monument by Chantrey, representing the last moments of David Pike Watts. In the churchyard are two fine Saxon crosses.

The road to the left in the village reaches the foot of Dovedale in three-quarters of a mile at Thorpe Mill (p. 142).

Tissington

two miles north-east of Thorpe, is an idyllic little village with a manor Hall, a church with Norman doorway and font, a village green surrounded by trees, and bright grey cottages.
From the early days of spring to the close of autumn the spot is one that lovers of nature and simplicity may visit in full assurance of gratification. But by reason of the observance of the old custom of **Well-Dressing,** there are a few

days of the year when Tissington's charms are increased beyond compute.

Among Nature's gifts to the parish are five wells—Hall Well, Hand's Well, Yew Tree Well, Town Well and Coffin Well. These are perennial springs issuing from the limestone and, although cold, somewhat resembling the tepid waters of Buxton and Matlock Bath. According to tradition, the flow of the springs continued at a time when all the others in the neighbourhood became dry. In gratitude for the great blessing afforded to the village, the wells were tastefully decorated with the best that could be culled from garden, field and hedgerow. This became an annual festival, held on Ascension Day, though the preparations begin long before the day. A picture of religious significance is designed for each well, and is then worked out by individual flower-petals pressed on to wet clay, the whole being mounted upon a large wooden frame. The effect is a brilliant mosaic, and must involve immense labour to achieve. Over each well is placed an appropriate scripture text also worked out in petals. On the festal day there is a church service at 11 a.m. Afterwards the round of the wells is made in procession from the church, a pause being made at each well while hymns are sung and prayers said. The decorations remain till after the following Sunday.

Tissington Hall, the fine Jacobean mansion of the FitzHerberts, was erected in 1609. An older hall existed before that date, but on the other side of the road, where no trace remains.

ASHBOURNE AND GEORGE ELIOT'S COUNTRY

ASHBOURNE

Access from Matlock, Buxton and Derby by bus or coach. Road route from Matlock *viâ* Cromford and Wirksworth; from Buxton by the main Ashbourne highway *viâ* Alsop-en-le-Dale.

Angling.—*See* p. 16.

Banks. — *Barclays*, St. John Street; *Lloyds*, Compton Street; *Westminster*, Church Street; *Williams Deacon's*, Dig Street.

Churches and Chapels, with hours of service on Sundays:—
St. Oswald's Parish Church, Church Street, and *St. John's*, Buxton Road —both at 11 and 6.30.

Roman Catholic (All Saints'), Belle Vue Road—8.45, 11 and 6.30.

Congregational, Derby Road, *Methodist*, Church Street and Station Street—all at 10.45 and 6.30.

Elim Mission Hall, South Street—11, 2 and 6.30.

Early Closing Day.—Wednesday.

Golf.—The 9-hole course of the *Ashbourne Golf Club* is at Clifton, 1½ miles from the town.

Hotels.—*See* Introduction, p. 10.

Population.—5,656.

Post Offices.—Compton Street and Market Place.

The town is referred to as *Esseburne* in the Domesday Book, and there are records of markets held in the reign of Henry III. The thirteenth-century cross now in the church is probably the one which stood in the market place. A fire destroyed the town in 1252.

In 1644 there was a skirmish between Parliamentary and Royalist troops and the following year Charles I attended service at the parish church on his flight to Wales. A century later, Charles's unfortunate great-grandson, Charles Edward Stuart, visited Ashbourne on his journey to and on his retreat from Derby, and proclaimed his father, the Pretender, King of Great Britain and Ireland. On that occasion Sir Brooke Boothby was the owner of Ashbourne Hall, and he and his family were unceremoniously dispossessed of their home, which was occupied by the prince and his officers.

The connection of Cotton and Izaak Walton, and before them of the Cokaynes and the Boothbys, with Ashbourne are its chief literary glories. Later, Dr. Johnson frequently visited it when wearied of his favourite " walk down Fleet Street." On such occasions he was always the welcome guest of his friend, Dr. Taylor, whose house, notable for its stone portico, is still to be seen. It is the last house but one (No. 70) on the left-hand side of the main street, which ends at the east gate of the churchyard. It was being partly rebuilt during Johnson's visit in 1784, to his great disgust.

Writing to Mrs. Thrale, in July, 1771, Johnson describes the town as " Ashbourne in the Peak." " Let not the barren name of the Peak terrify you," he adds, " I have never wanted strawberries and cream." It was the landlady of the *Green Man*—now the *Green Man and Black's Head*—who, so Boswell tells us in his *Life*, promised him " her sincerest prayers for his happiness in time and in a blessed eternity " if he would only be kind enough to mention her house favourably to his friends! The Black's Head, a fierce-looking effigy set up on a signboard across the main street, was the sign of a house of which the business was taken over by the *Green Man*.

It was the pealing of the bells in Ashbourne Church that inspired Tom Moore to the writing of one of his most exquisite songs, *Those Evening Bells*, and in the closing verse he alludes not only to the bells, but to the dells of the neighbouring Dovedale—

> " And so 'twill be when I am gone,
> That tuneful peal will still ring on,
> While other bards shall walk these dells,
> And sing your praise, sweet evening bells."

Ashbourne is built in a fertile valley, a mile and a half east of the Dove, with well-wooded hills protecting three of its sides, and with an extensive outlook over the valley through which the river flows to the south. The straight main street runs eastward from the Parish Church past the War Memorial Arch and Recreation Grounds, continuing through Cokayne Avenue, to join up with the common land of Ashbourne Green. The Recreation Grounds once formed part of the Ashbourne Hall estate, but of this there remains only the Hall, part of which houses the County Library (open *Tues., Thurs., and Fri.*).

The Parish Church

is the chief object not only in the town but in the neighbourhood. Boswell spoke of the beautiful building as " one of the largest and most luminous churches that I have seen in any town of the same size," while George Eliot, going much farther, described it as " the finest mere parish church in the Kingdom."

The church was consecrated in 1241. It occupies the site of a church mentioned in Domesday, and is dedicated to St. Oswald, king and martyr, who is represented by a modern red sandstone statue outside, at the western end. Chiefly Early English, with additions and alterations in the Decorated, Perpendicular and Tudor periods, the building consists of chancel, transepts and nave, with a south aisle, evidently a later addition. The central tower supports a beautiful octagonal spire 215 feet high, pierced with twenty dormer lights, and known as the " pride of the Peak." In the belfry are the bells that charmed the poet Moore.

The **Nave** contains coloured windows of which the most attractive is the " Turnbull " window on the south side. It is by Christopher

Whall, and was inserted in 1905. The wearied St. Cecilia has fallen asleep at the organ, but angels carry on the creation of song and praise. In the north-west corner will be seen memorials to the fallen in the two world wars.

In the **North Transept** on the west side near the door is a priceless lancet window of thirteenth-century glass, representing scenes connected with the Nativity. In the adjoining **Boothby Chapel** are fine windows, an ancient aumbry, memorials of the Cokayne family (fourteenth to seventeenth centuries) and also memorials of the Boothbys and the Bradbournes. The white marble recumbent effigy by Thomas Banks, R.A., of Penelope Boothby excites the admiration of every visitor, and gave Chantrey, it is said, inspiration for his sculpture of the sleeping children in Lichfield Cathedral. It has inscriptions in English, French, Italian and Latin. Penelope Boothby died in 1791 at the age of 5 years and 11 months. Her portrait, when she was little more than three, by Sir Joshua Reynolds, is one of the most famous and attractive of his pictures of children. In 1859 it was bought by the Earl of Dudley for 1,100 guineas and was purchased in 1885 by Mr. Thwaites for £20,000. What is said of the child's marble effigy adds interest to the fact that her portrait led to the production of another celebrated picture—the " Cherry Ripe " of Millais, who thus painted little Miss Talmage after she had been to a fancy dress ball as " Penelope."

In the **South Transept** is a large " Te Deum " window by Hardmans. Beyond the screen is the ancient chapel of St. Oswald, a particularly fine Perpendicular window, and the dedication brass (1241), supposed to be the oldest in existence. The registers date from 1538; the font is the original thirteenth-century one.

The **Choir** is remarkable for its fine Perpendicular east window by Kempe. It contains the arms of John of Gaunt, the Duchy of Lancaster, and families connected with the neighbourhood. On the south side are coupled lancet windows containing stained glass representing the history of David and Goliath. It attracts special notice because Ruskin described the artist's efforts as " a disgrace to a penny edition of *Jack the Giant Killer*." On the north side of the chancel is a canopied tomb with crocketed pinnacles.

A feature of the town is the number of its **Almshouses.** Adjoining the churchyard are some due to the charity of Nicholas Spalden. In Church Street, Owfield's and Pegg's Almshouses adjoin; in a recess on the south side of the same street are almshouses for clergymen's widows; and another group adjoins the Congregational church.

The former **Grammar School** situated on the north side of Church Street received its charter in 1585. The present co-educational school is housed in a modern building at the end of the town.

On the steep Buxton Road, St. John's Church is a stone building with a square tower erected by a local benefactor last century.

Shrove Tuesday Football

A description of Ashbourne would be incomplete without mention of Shrove Tuesday Football. Magisterial powers, exercised again and again, with summonses and prosecutions, have proved quite inadequate to suppress this carnival, and the game has received Royal approval, the Duke of Windsor, when Prince of Wales, having "thrown up the ball" in 1928. Not only do the inhabitants of Ashbourne take part in the "game," but the neighbouring villages supply strong reinforcements. It is a "clearing-house" day, when old scores are paid off and old accounts adjusted. On the following morning the local chemists find a phenomenal demand for arnica and surgical plasters. The combatants are known as "The Uppards" and "The Downards." Anyone born north of the dividing line plays with the "Uppards," while those born south side with the "Downards."

At two o'clock punctually the ball—a large leathern sphere stuffed with cork shavings—is thrown up on a little knoll in the centre of Shaw Croft, usually by some prominent person, to the strains of the National Anthem, Rule Britannia, and other patriotic airs. Then the "fun" waxes fast and furious. "The Uppards" play by Park Road, the Park, and across to Sturston Mill. "The Downards" play over and under the Bridge, past Compton Street, the Paddock and across Tomlinson's Fields to Clifton Mill. The goals are a mile and a half apart. Sometimes the ball is reduced in the rough and tumble of the scrimmage to a mere scrap of leather. But when that tiny scrap touches the mill wheel it scores.

Ashbourne to Dovedale. The best route is to take the road to the left at the upper end of the Market Place, turning right in about 200 yards to cross a ridge into the pastoral valley of the *Bentley Brook*. The road then works round the southern end of a long ridge to the wider valley of the *Dove*. Before reaching **Mapleton** (or Mappleton, as it is sometimes called), Bunster Hill and Thorpe Cloud, those guardians of the southern end of Dovedale, have come into view. Mapleton is a pleasing little village with a very curious church. The road for Dovedale goes straight on and up, giving good views over the Dove to the neighbouring *Manifold*. Turn to the left by the *Dog and Partridge Hotel*, and pass the entrance to the *Peveril of the Peak Hotel* to reach the quiet village of **Thorpe** (about 4 miles from Ashbourne), whence the continuation to Dovedale is described on page 142.

GEORGE ELIOT'S COUNTRY

Ashbourne is at the edge of the "George Eliot Country," a district that is well worth exploring quite apart from its literary interest. For the most part the "George Eliot Country" lies in Staffordshire, the "Loamshire" of *Adam Bede*, as Derbyshire is its "Stonyshire," Dovedale its "Eagle Dale," and the mountains of the Peak its "barren hills."

Ellastone is the " Hayslope " described in the second chapter of *Adam Bede,* and was the early home of Robert Evans, " George Eliot's " father. The family residence was the two-storeyed cottage standing by the side of the road leading to Wootton, and is easily recognized by the curious pinnacles which surmount the garden wall.

The " Donnithorne Arms " in the story is the *Bromley Arms* at the cross roads, " Oakbourne " has been identified as Ashbourne, " Snowfield " as Wirksworth (4 miles south of Matlock), and " Norbourne " as Norbury. " Donnithorne Chase " is supposed to be either Wootton Hall, a mile to the north of Ellastone, or Calwich Abbey, half a mile to the east.

Norbury

the novelist's " Norbourne," is some 4 miles south-west of Ashbourne. Its particular treasure is **St. Mary's Church.**

It was built between 1370 and 1380. and restored by the Clowes family in 1899. Seated on the summit of a hill, its tower is seen for a long distance and commands a wide landscape; but the edifice is chiefly noteworthy for its large windows and the beauty of their early stained glass, of which Dr. Cox remarks, " There are not six parish churches in the kingdom that have so fine and extensive a display." The FitzHerberts (Lords of Norbury) owned the Hall from the twelfth century until recently; and the Church contains their tombs, brasses, etc. One of the most notable is the monument of Sir Anthony FitzHerbert, a judge in the days of Henry VIII. He is represented clad in full judicial robes, and his wife wears a wonderful heraldic mantle. The earliest of the tombs is that of Sir Henry FitzHerbert, who lived two hundred years before the days of the judge. Remains of the manor house are near the church.

Within a mile to the north-west of Norbury is—

Ellastone

the " Hayslope " of *Adam Bede,* and a delightful unspoiled village. The village boasts a fine old Perpendicular church, the embattled tower of which is a familiar landmark. Within is the altar-tomb of St. Richard Fleetwood, lord of Calwich in the days of Charles II.

Calwich Abbey, half a mile east of Ellastone, but now demolished, was a modern residence, occupying the site of an oratory founded in the reign of Stephen. There formerly stood a house in which Handel composed part of *The Messiah.*

A mile and a half north-west of Ellastone is the village of **Wootton.** In a local epigram it appears as " Wootton under-Weaver, where God came neever." The **Weaver Hills,** under which it stands, are a limestone range, the southern-most outpost of the Peak District and hence of the whole Pennine Range.

Wootton Lodge, a parapeted mansion, about a mile and a half west of Ellastone, was besieged during the Civil War (*see* p. 134).

Mayfield

The highway between Ellastone and Ashbourne crosses the Dove here by the **Hanging Bridge,** an ancient stone structure of five narrow arches reconstructed in 1936. Mayfield Church is interesting for its many Norman details, chief of which is the arch of the south door; the west door, by the way, still bears marks of bullets fired at it by the Pretender's soldiers in 1745. But the chief attraction of the village is the cottage wherein Moore resided with his wife " Bessie " from the summer of 1813 to March, 1817. Here he wrote *Lalla Rookh* and other poems, including *Those Evening Bells,* and here too, he was visited by the banker-poet Rogers. In the churchyard lies buried Moore's daughter, Olivia Byron, who according to tradition was given her second name after Byron, a friend of Moore, and who acted as the child's godfather. Close by is an ancient cross removed here from the village.

INDEX

Where more than one reference is given, the first is the principal.

INDEX